Reed Ne

Common Insects

of New Zealand

He koha nāku ki ōku hoa papai,
te whānau McLeod
— John, Kay, Andrew, Ian ā Fiona.

Reed New Zealand Nature Series

Common Insects

of New Zealand

Brian Parkinson

Cover photograph: German Wasp
Title page: European Earwig

Established in 1907, Reed Publishing (NZ) Ltd
is New Zealand's largest book publisher, with over 300 titles in print.

For details on all these books visit our website:
www.reed.co.nz

Published by Reed Books, a division of Reed Publishing (NZ) Ltd,
39 Rawene Rd, Birkenhead, Auckland 10.
Associated companies, branches and representatives throughout the world.

This book is copyright. Except for the purpose of fair reviewing,
no part of this publication may be reproduced or transmitted in any
form or by any means, electronic or mechanical, including photocopying,
recording, or any information storage and retrieval system, without
permission in writing from the publisher. Infringers of copyright render
themselves liable to prosecution.

© 2001 Brian Parkinson
The author asserts his moral rights in the work.
© 2001 Rod Morris — all photographs except where otherwise credited below.
All photographs are property of the photographers.
Illustrations on page 9 by Cuni de Graaf.

Brian Chudleigh: Species Nos: 2, 8, 9 (all), 10, 12, 20 (left-hand page),
21 (top), 22 (left-hand page), 36, 52
Leonie Clunie, Landcare Research, Auckland: Species No. 26
Andrew Crowe: Species No. 24
Don Horne: Species No. 3
Brian Patrick: Species Nos: 1, 37, 46
Graham Walker, Crop & Food Research, Auckland: Species No. 21 (lower)

ISBN 0 7900 0786 X
First published 2001

Edited by Carolyn Lagahetau
Designed by Graeme Leather
Scanning and Prepress by i2i Imaging
Printed in Singapore

Contents

Introduction   7
What is an insect?   8
How an insect is named   10
Insects and us   11

		SPECIES NO.
Spiny-gilled Mayfly	*Coloburiscus humeralis*	1
Australian Damselfly	*Ischnura aurora aurora*	2
Blue Damselfly	*Austrolestes colensonis*	3
Redcoat Damselfly	*Xanthocnemis zealandica*	4
Bush Giant Dragonfly	*Uropetala carovei*	5
Large Green Stonefly	*Stenoperla prasina*	6
Black Cockroach	*Platyzosteria novaeseelandiae*	7
Gisborne Cockroach	*Drymaplaneta semivitta*	8
Praying Mantis	*Orthodera novaezealandiae*	9
Springbok Mantis	*Miomantis caffra*	10
European Earwig	*Forficula auricularia*	11
Shore Earwig	*Anisolabis littorea*	12
Auckland Tree Weta	*Hemideina thoracica*	13
Cave Weta	*Gymnoplectron* spp.	14
Black Field Cricket	*Teleogryllus commodus*	15
Katydid	*Caedicia simplex*	16
Migratory Locust	*Locusta migratoria*	17
Prickly Stick Insect	*Acanthoxyla prasina*	18
Backswimmer	*Anisops assimilis*	19
Clapping Cicada	*Amphipsalta cingulata*	20
Cabbage Aphid	*Brevicoryne brassicae*	21
Green Vegetable Bug	*Nezara viridula*	22
Passionvine Hopper	*Scolypopa australis*	23
Watermeasurer	*Hydrometra risbeci*	24
Waterboatman	*Sigara arguta*	25
Greenhouse Thrip	*Heliothrips haemorrhoidalis*	26
Dobsonfly	*Archichauliodes diversus*	27

		SPECIES NO.
Antlion	*Weeleus acutus*	28
Carabid Beetle	*Megadromus capito*	29
Cosmopolitan Diving Beetle	*Rhantus pulverosus*	30
Devil's Coachhorse Beetle	*Creophilus oculatus*	31
Tiger Beetle	*Neocicindela tuberculata*	32
Manuka Beetle	*Pyronota festiva*	33
Huhu Beetle	*Prionoplus reticularis*	34
Click Beetle	*Conoderus exsul*	35
Steelblue Ladybird	*Orcus chalybeus*	36
Elephant Weevil	*Rhyncodes ursus*	37
Giraffe Weevil	*Lasiorhynchus barbicornis*	38
Cat Flea	*Ctenocephalides felis*	39
Vigilant Mosquito	*Culex pervigilans*	40
Sandfly	*Austrosimulium australense*	41
Australian Soldierfly	*Exaireta spinigera*	42
Crane Fly	*Holorusia novarae*	43
Golden-haired Blowfly	*Calliphora laemica*	44
New Zealand Blue Blowfly	*Calliphora quadrimaculata*	45
Caddisfly	*Hydrobiosis parumbripennis*	46
White Butterfly	*Pieris rapae*	47
Monarch Butterfly	*Danaus plexippus*	48
Common Copper	*Lycaena salustius*	49
German Wasp	*Vespula germanica*	50
Common Wasp	*Vespula vulgaris*	51
Australian Paper Wasp	*Polistes tasmaniensis humilis*	52
Honey Bee	*Apis mellifera*	53
Bumblebee	*Bombus terrestris*	54
Southern Ant	*Monomorium antarcticum*	55

Index of common names   92
Index of Maori names   93
Index of scientific names   94

Introduction

This book is intended to cover all of the common insects that an interested observer is likely to encounter in New Zealand, either because they are conspicuous like the butterflies, irritating like ants and wasps, or they are significant garden pests like thrips and vegetable bugs.

Entomologists (the scientists who study insects) arrange insects in the order in which they evolved, starting from the most primitive which are insects like the bristletails, silverfish, mayflies and dragonflies, through to the most advanced insects like the bees, wasps, moths and ants.

Accordingly, this book is arranged to cover our common insects in this taxonomic order, as listed below, starting from the mayflies and running through to the ants.

Insect Order	Meaning	Approximate number of species worldwide	New Zealand examples
Collembola	sticky peg	6000	Springtail
Thysanura	bristletails	370	Silverfish
Ephemeroptera	living for a day	2100	Mayfly
Odonata	toothed flies	5500	Dragonfly
Plecoptera	wickerwork wings	2000	Stonefly
Blattodea	avoiding light	3700	Cockroach
Isoptera	equal wings	2300	Termites
Mantodea	prophet-like	1800	Mantis
Dermaptera	leather wings	1800	Earwig
Orthoptera	straight wings	20,500	Weta
Phasmatodea	ghost-like	2500	Stick insect
Pscoptera	milled wings	3200	Book lice
Phthiraptera	louse wings	3000	Head lice
Hemiptera	half wings	82,000	Cicada
Thysanoptera	fringed wings	5000	Thrips
Megaloptera	large wings	250	Dobsonfly
Neuroptera	net-veined wings	5000	Antlion
Coleoptera	hard wings	400,000	Beetles
Siphonaptera	wingless tubes	3000	Fleas
Diptera	two wings	120,000	Flies
Trichoptera	hairy wings	10,000	Caddisfly
Lepidoptera	scaly wings	1,503,000	Butterfly
Hymenoptera	membrane wings	130,000	Bee

What is an insect?

The word 'insect' comes from the creatures' Latin name *insectum*, which means 'notched' and refers to the animals' indented or divided body. Entomologists define an insect as having:

- three body parts: the head, thorax and abdomen;
- three pairs of legs;
- a single or double pair of wings.

The length given for each insect species is the distance from the head to the tip of the abdomen of an average example and does not include either the antennae or legs.

There is a tendency to lump a lot of smallish creatures under the title of insect. However, many of these animals are not insects at all. Spiders and ticks, for example, belong to another group, the Arachnida, and in any event have four pairs of legs; millipedes and centipedes are separated out into a group of their own named Myriapoda and slaters or woodlice belong to the order Crustacea.

However, as with all rules, there are exceptions. Many of our insects, including our best known example, the weta, are flightless despite being descendants of flying ancestors. Also, the description sometimes leaves something to be desired, as the early life stages of many insects look nothing like the eventual adults.

NEW ZEALAND WETA GROUPS SHOWING INSECT PARTS

TUSKED WETA

Antennae

Cerci

LEG
Femur
Tibia
Tarsus

GIANT WETA

Abdomen
Head
Foreleg

GROUND WETA

COMMON WETA

Thorax

CAVE WETA

Hindlegs
Midlegs

How an insect is named

Insects are often named for their habitat, like the Grapevine Moth, or for details of their behaviour, as in the case of the Praying Mantis. The problem arises when we have more than one example of a certain type of insect. One example of this is that posed by the relatively recent arrival in New Zealand of a second species of Praying Mantis. Naming the new arrival the Springbok Mantis solved this, but this name does not mean all that much to someone from overseas, even someone from South Africa.

This is where the scientific name comes in. Once the animal or plant has been recognised as being different from all other related or similar animals or plants, each is given a scientific name.

The scientific name is in two parts:

- Firstly, the name of the genus of the animal or plant is given. This is roughly the equivalent of our surnames. The genus gives the general classification for the animal or plant and shows its relationship to other similar species.

- Secondly, the animal or plant is given its species name, which is similar to our Christian or given names. This name is often chosen by, or on behalf of, the scientist or naturalist who first discovered the animal or plant, or by the person who realised the species was new to science.

Although this does not always happen, ideally, the scientific name should describe a characteristic of the organism being named. For example, the scientific name of the Redcoat Damselfly is *Xanthocnemis zealandica*. *Xanthocnemis* means 'yellow legs' and *zealandica* indicates that this damselfly is from New Zealand.

Insects and us

As insects first appeared on earth some 400 million years ago, there has been plenty of time for the evolutionary processes to have produced the myriad forms of insect life that we see around us today.

At the same time, some insects like dragonflies, cockroaches and mayflies early on evolved into forms that, being well suited to their environment, have remained largely unchanged since they first appeared on earth. Indeed, it has been claimed that the cockroach has such remarkable powers of survival (including the capacity to withstand radiation ten times higher than that which would prove fatal to us) that it is likely to be around long after humans as a species have become extinct.

Insects are the most numerous group of animals on earth. About a million species have so far been named and entomologists estimate that between five and ten million remain to be classified. This compares with around 4600 mammals and some 9700 birds.

Insects live just about anywhere — on the ground, on trees and shrubs, under ground and in caves, in fresh water and salty water, and on, and in, other animals. There are blood-suckers and plant-suckers, book-chewers and bark-chewers, and wood-borers and wood-gnawers, together with a host of other even more specialised feeders.

In your own back yard, in an area of one square metre you could find up to 2000 insects. Take a close look at some of these 'critters' and their fascinating lifestyles.

1 Spiny-gilled Mayfly/Piri Wai
Coloburiscus humeralis Order: EPHEMEROPTERA
Family: SIPHLONURIDAE

Appearance • All mayflies are easily distinguished from other aquatic insects by their thread-like tail appendages and by the way they hold their fragile, transparent, net-veined wings vertically over their bodies.

Spiny-gilled Mayfly larvae lurk under stones wherever there is any water movement. They can be distinguished from the larvae of other mayfly species by the seven pairs of forked spiny gills they carry on their abdomens.

Development • Unlike the larvae of other mayflies that graze on vegetation, those of the *Coloburiscus* genus filter fine particles from the water. As the name of their order indicates, their life is ephemeral, lasting at the most a few days, which they spend lurking in the shelter of shoreline vegetation, flying out over the water at dawn and dusk to mate. During this time they do not eat, as their sole purpose is to breed. As a consequence of this, the mouthparts of the adults are much reduced. After laying her eggs, the female dies.

Distribution and Habitat • Found along any moving river or stream throughout New Zealand.

Adult body length • 15 mm.

Remarks • Other common mayfly species that are found in New Zealand are the Sucker-gilled Mayfly, *Deleatidium myzobranchia*, the Double-gilled Mayfly, *Zephlebia versicolor*, and the Swimming Mayfly, *Nesameletus ornatus*.

2 Australian Damselfly/Tiemiemi
Ischnura aurora aurora
Order: ODONATA
Family: COENAGRIONIDAE

Appearance • Damselflies can readily be distinguished from dragonflies. Damselflies fold their wings over their backs when at rest, while dragonflies keep their wings extended.

Development • The male seizes the female soon after she emerges from her final larval stage and mates with her. Eggs are laid on the emergent stems of aquatic plants where they hatch in two to three weeks. The carnivorous larvae are free-swimming and the larval stage lasts about a year.

Distribution and Habitat • The Australian Damselfly is the smallest damselfly found in New Zealand. In the North Island it is also one of the commonest. It is also found on many Pacific Islands, as well as in parts of Asia, ranging from Pakistan in the west, to as far east as Tahiti. It is a relatively recent arrival from Australia, first recorded in New Zealand in 1926. So far, it has only colonised the North Island. It is a familiar sight in patches of vegetation along the quiet stretches of water that it favours. The Australian Damselfly is one of the few damselflies to breed in mangrove swamps.

Adult body length • 25 mm.

Remarks • The Australian Damselfly is sometimes called the Gossamer Damselfly.

Blue Damselfly/Kekewai
Austrolestes colensonis

Order: ODONATA
Family: LESTIDAE

3

Appearance • The Blue Damselfly is the largest of our damselflies. It can be distinguished from other damselfly species found here, both by its size and its colour. The males are blue and the females are bright green. These colours tend to be fairly dull in the morning, getting brighter as the day warms up. The male's habit of perching with its wings held at right angles to its body is another diagnostic feature.

Development • The males seize the emerging females and the pair then fly in tandem to nearby aquatic vegetation where they remain joined together while the female, sometimes completely submerged, lays her eggs.

Distribution and Habitat • Blue damselflies are common along any stretch of still water edged by vegetation, such as rushes, sedges and reeds. The damselfly needs such vegetation for depositing its eggs. The Blue Damselfly occurs from Northland south to Southland. It is widespread throughout much of New Zealand except for the Kermadec Islands.

Adult body length • 45 mm.

Resting male Blue Damselfly.

Redcoat Damselfly/Kihitara
Xanthocnemis zealandica

Order: ODONATA
Family: COENAGRIONIDAE

Appearance • The common name, Red Damselfly, is not truly correct, as although the male is red with black markings, the female varies in colour between red and bronze.

Development • Eggs are laid in slits that the female cuts in aquatic plants. The larvae are generally slow-moving, swimming with slow side-to-side undulations. When sedentary they regulate their colours to match their backgrounds. They are often covered with reddish mites such as *Eylais waikawae* and *Arrenurus rotoensis*.

Distribution and Habitat • The Redcoat Damselfly is the most widespread of our damselflies. It can be found in any suitable habitat such as over riparian vegetation and near small ponds, tarns and slow-flowing streams throughout mainland New Zealand and the Chatham Islands.

Adult body length • 32 mm.

The Redcoat Damselfly has been in New Zealand long enough to have evolved into a number of different species. These are variously called the Kauri Redcoat Damselfly, *X. sobrina*, the Chatham Redcoat Damselfly, *X. tuanuii*, and the Alpine Redcoat Damselfly, *X. sinclairii*.

A recently emerged male Redcoat Damselfly.

5 Bush Giant Dragonfly/Kakapowai
Uropetala carovei

Order: ODONATA
Family: PETALURIDAE

Appearance • A large, blackish dragonfly with a wingspan of up to 125 mm and a distinctive yellow-striped abdomen. The head is large and highly mobile, the body is slender, the antennae are short and the eyes are large and compound. The flight is fast and direct.

Development • The females lay their eggs in vegetation in boggy areas, or along the muddy margins of small streams. The larvae are fairly sluggish with well-developed compound eyes. They do not have gills, but instead breathe by pumping water in and out of their recta. They construct long burrows in mud, clay or peat, with a resting chamber at the end, emerging at night to catch nocturnal insects at the burrow mouth. The larvae go through a series of moults and the adolescent period can last as long as six years before the adult form emerges.

Distribution and Habitat • The Bush Giant Dragonfly is New Zealand's largest and most spectacular species. It is widespread throughout the North Island but has patchy distribution in the South Island, being found in various parts of Nelson and Marlborough, on the West Coast and in Southland. The Bush Giant Dragonfly is not too particular about its habitat requirements. It has been found along bush margins, in tree tops and over scrub. It hunts a variety of insect prey including bees, wasps and butterflies.

Adult body length • 85 mm.

Remarks • There is a very similar species to the Bush Giant Dragonfly, the Mountain Giant Dragonfly, *U. chiltoni*. The Mountain Giant Dragonfly is generally confined to tussock grasslands in the South Island high country. It differs by having a yellow patch on its upper lip or labrum.

Also known as the Devil's Darning Needle.

Dragonflies are poorly represented in New Zealand, with only seventeen species having so far been recorded out of the several thousand species that occur worldwide.

6 Large Green Stonefly/Ngarongaro Wai
Stenoperla prasina

Order: PLECOPTERA
Family: EUSTHENIIDAE

Appearance • Stoneflies are long, narrow insects and are either poor fliers or flightless. The Large Green Stonefly is one of the largest stoneflies found in New Zealand, as well as being the greenest in colour. Most other New Zealand stoneflies are either brown or grey.

Development • The female Large Green Stonefly lays between 100 and 1000 eggs, which can take up to a year to hatch. The larvae are commonly found along stony streams but seem to favour the lower reaches, where they prey on the larvae of other insects, particularly those of mayflies.

Distribution and Habitat • From coastal to alpine zones throughout mainland New Zealand. Unlike the short-lived mayflies, stoneflies live for several months. They favour shady areas along the banks of clear, stony and relatively fast-flowing streams. However, as they are not strong fliers and they spend much of their time lurking in the vegetation.

Adult body length • 30 mm.

Remarks • There are about 2000 species of stoneflies worldwide and just over 50 are found in New Zealand. Many of the New Zealand species are flightless, which is why they are sometimes called stoners. Other common New Zealand stoneflies include the Long-tailed Stonefly, *Zelandoperla maculata*, and the Short-tailed Stonefly, *Aucklandobius trivacuata*.

Stoneflies are sufficiently different from other insects to be given their own order, Plecoptera. This translates as 'wickerwork wings', a feature that can be readily distinguished when a flighted adult is closely studied.

Adult Large Green Stonefly.

Black Cockroach/Kekerengu

7 *Platyzosteria novaeseelandiae*   Order: BLATTODEA
Family: BLATTIDAE

Appearance • Blackish-coloured, flightless, flat-backed and crepuscular with long, thin, constantly twitching antennae and long, spiky legs well developed for running.

Development • The female produces a hard egg case called an ootheca, which contains up to 40 eggs. This is usually deposited in ground litter and the emergent nymphs go through about six moults before attaining adulthood.

Distribution • Widespread throughout warmer parts of the country. Although normally found outdoors it sometimes ventures into houses. The Black Cockroach displays typical cockroach behaviour, being exclusively nocturnal and skulking around under rocks and logs and in litter during the day. It will feed on anything vaguely edible, polluting what it doesn't eat with its excrement.

Adult body length • 22 mm.

Remarks • Although cockroaches are well known to many householders, they are almost invariably one of the introduced species. There are very few native species of cockroaches in New Zealand, the Black Cockroach being probably the best known of these.

The Black Cockroach is sometimes known as the Black Stinkroach.

The Black Cockroach is related to the introduced species generally known as the Gisborne Cockroach. However, unlike the Gisborne Cockroach, the Black Cockroach is flightless.

However poorly you might regard them, cockroaches are born survivors. They have been around for hundreds of millions of years and could be around long after humans disappear.

Adult Black Cockroach.

8 Gisborne Cockroach
Drymaplaneta semivitta

Order: BLATTODEA
Family: BLATTIDAE

Appearance • Can be distinguished from other introduced cockroaches by its larger size, darker colouration and yellowish markings on the outer edge of the thorax.

Development • Development is similar to that of the Black Cockroach, except that the ootheca, the egg case, is often deposited inside buildings.

Distribution and Habitat • Why this cockroach is called the Gisborne Cockroach is a bit of a mystery, as it first arrived in New Zealand at Tauranga in 1954, probably in a log shipment, so Tauranga should really get the honour of having this insect as its namesake. From Tauranga it has now spread over much of the North Island. Although in its native West Australia it is primarily an outdoor insect, frequenting logs and fallen vegetation, in New Zealand it is often found indoors, although it is probably inadvertently brought inside with firewood.

Adult body length • 25 mm.

Remarks • Like other cockroaches, the Gisborne Cockroach will eat just about anything, even cardboard and the labels of cans and jars. They discharge liquid from their mouths to soften their food. The liquid is also a medium for bacteria.

The one positive thing that can be said about cockroaches is that if you do have them you are unlikely to have bedbugs!

The other common introduced cockroach, the German Cockroach, *Drymaplaneta semivitta* is smaller, is a drab brown colour and has wings that can be easily seen.

9 Praying Mantis/Whe
Orthodera novaezealandiae Order: MANTODEA
Family: MANTIDAE

Appearance • A large, green and distinctively shaped insect with large compound eyes, a mobile head and front legs held out in the diagnostic 'praying' posture.

Development • In the late summer, the female Praying Mantis becomes very heavy with eggs. She seeks out a suitable spot, such as a branch or a wall, to construct her zipper-like egg case, which is known as an ootheca. In this she lays several hundred eggs. The emergent hatchlings take about a year, during which they go through several moults, to reach maturity.

Distribution and Habitat • Once widespread throughout mainland New Zealand but now displaced from more northerly areas by the Springbok Mantis, a recent immigrant.

Adult body length • 40 mm.

Remarks • The word 'mantis' is Greek and means 'prophet'. This insect's familiar 'praying' stance (a source of fascination to most children), is merely a device for catching insects. Some observers have suggested it might be better if it was called the 'Preying Mantis'.

Although the Praying Mantis can fly, in general it prefers not to. Instead, it likes to lie in wait for any prey that ventures close enough for it to grab. It is not too particular about what it eats and any insect that is small enough is fair game. The female is quite capable of even eating its own mate.

The Praying Mantis is also found in Australia.

ABOVE: New Zealand Praying Mantis laying eggs.

RIGHT: New Zealand Praying Mantis eating Passionvine Hopper.

LEFT: New Zealand Praying Mantises emerging from egg case.

10 Springbok Mantis
Miomantis caffra

Order: MANTODEA
Family: MANTIDAE

Appearance • Similar to the Praying Mantis. However, the Springbok Mantis tends to be brown to pink in colour, while the Praying Mantis is green.

Development • Around cities like Auckland, its distinctive frothy egg-cases are now a familiar sight, liberally scattered along the more sheltered parts of buildings such as under eaves. The female Springbok Mantis, like other mantids, has the charming habit of eating her mate after the act of mating. The young look like large ants, with upwardly pointing abdomens.

Distribution and Habitat • As its name implies, the Springbok Mantis immigrated here from South Africa. This has only happened in the last 30 years or so, but in this relatively short space of time it has colonised a fairly sizable chunk of the North Island. In so doing it has largely displaced our native Praying Mantis from these areas.

Adult body length • 40 mm.

Remarks • This species is capable of consuming prey as large as fully grown Monarch Butterfly caterpillars.

Female Springbok Mantis eating male after mating.

European Earwig
Forficula auricularia

Order: DERMAPTERA
Family: FORFICULIDAE

Appearance • Earwigs have rather strangely shaped short and leathery wings that early observers thought were similar in shape to the human ear. The insect was thus called the earwing, which over time has become corrupted to earwig. There is absolutely no truth in the belief that the earwig sometimes crawls into human ears.

Development • For an insect, the European Earwig is a suprisingly devoted mother, carefully tending her eggs and cleaning them of any fungus or mildew.

Distribution and Habitat • The European Earwig arrived in New Zealand with some of the earliest European settlers, and has since then become widely established in many parts of the country.

Adult body length • 15 mm.

Remarks • The European Earwig is not too fussy about what it eats. It does, however, seem to have a preference for stone- and pip-fruits, sometimes causing considerable damage to peach, apricot and nectarine orchards.

Adult male European Earwig.

12 Shore Earwig/Mata
Anisolabis littorea

Order: DERMAPTERA
Family: FORFICULIDAE

Appearance • Similar to the European Earwig, but the Shore Earwig is flightless, larger, darker in colour and often has a yellow band at the back of its thorax. The cerci, which are the pair of jointed appendages at the rear of the abdomen, have been adapted as pincers.

Development • Like the European Earwig, the Shore Earwig is a surprisingly devoted mother, carefully tending her eggs and keeping them clean of fungal infections. Once the eggs hatch she guards the young until they are big enough to fend for themselves, although she is not above eating them if times get tough.

Distribution and Habitat • If you chance to turn over a piece of driftwood or a large piece of kelp above the high-water mark while wandering along the beach in any suitable coastal areas of the North Island and in the South Island north of about Dunedin, you stand a very good chance of finding a Shore Earwig, which is New Zealand's native earwig. Here, it ekes out an existence, preying on small invertebrates such as sandhoppers. The Shore Earwig attacks the sandhoppers at speed, crushing its victims with its strong pincers.

Adult body length • 30 mm.

Remarks • Shore Earwigs are rather similar to the introduced species of earwigs in their habits and are not adverse to invading buildings and hunting down slaters, millipedes and other insects.

Shore Earwig with young.

13 Auckland Tree Weta/Tokoriro
Hemideina thoracica

Order: ORTHOPTERA
Family: STENOPELMATIDAE

Appearance • Similar in shape to other species of tree weta. However, the head of the Auckland Tree Weta is usually much darker than that of other species.

Development • Tree Weta live together in small groups called galleries, which are usually tunnels left in trees by the wood-boring larvae of beetles. Females can lay eggs at any time of the year, but seem to have a preference for April and May, when the ground has been softened by autumnal rains. The female descends to the ground, digs a hole with her ovipositor, then lays up to 200 eggs. The nymphs are smaller, paler versions of the adults. They go through several moults and take about a year to reach maturity.

Distribution and Habitat • This weta occurs throughout the northern North Island, north of a line running roughly between Mount Taranaki and northern Hawkes Bay. Despite a common belief held by many New Zealanders, New Zealand is not the only place weta are found. They also live in a number of overseas countries, but nowhere else have they evolved into the wealth of forms and varieties seen in New Zealand. Mostly vegetarian, weta spend the day hiding in nooks and crannies, emerging at night to feed on the foliage of plants such as mahoe and lacebark.

Adult body length • 65 mm.

Remarks • In the southern part of the North Island and in the northern and eastern parts of the South Island, this weta is replaced by the Wellington Tree Weta, *Hemideina crassidens*. The Wellington Tree Weta differs from the Auckland Tree Weta in that its head is brown and it has brown stripes on its abdomen.

Weta have been on earth since the Mesozoic era. Due to the absence of mammals in New Zealand, they took on the role filled by mammals in other parts of the world, becoming a sort of insectivorous rodent.

Being flightless, the Auckland Tree Weta has declined greatly in numbers since humans and introduced predators settled in New Zealand.

Adult male Auckland Tree Weta in threat posture.

14 Cave Weta/Weta Taipo
Gymnoplectron spp.

Order: ORTHOPTERA
Family: RHAPHIDOPHORIDAE

Appearance • Cave Weta differ from true weta in that they have smaller bodies and much longer legs and antennae. The hindlegs are, as with all Orthoptera, greatly enlarged.

Development • Similar to that of the Tree Weta, except that the eggs are laid in crevices rather than in the ground.

Distribution and Habitat • Although called Cave Weta, these insects are found in a wide variety of different habitats, ranging from culverts and tunnels to logs and crevices in large rocks.

Adult body length • 30 mm.

Remarks • Cave Weta are generally vegetarian but, as opportunists, they will make use of other foodstuffs when available. For example, two species of Cave Weta that live on the Chatham Islands, *Talitropsis crassicruris* and *Novoplectron serratum*, feed on dead seabirds. Although Cave Weta do congregate together in caves during the day, at night they feed by themselves.

There are about 50 species of Cave Weta in New Zealand. They are also found in other countries such as Chile, Australia and South Africa, where they go under such names as the Camel Cricket and Cave Cricket.

Female Wellington Cave Weta.

Black Field Cricket/Pihareinga
Teleogryllus commodus

Order: ORTHOPTERA
Family: GRYLLIDAE

15

Appearance • A medium-sized, shiny, blackish insect, with long antennae and prominent hindlegs, like other orthopterids.

Development • The female uses her ovipositor to lay her white, cigar-shaped eggs deep in the soil. The hatchlings look like miniature, wingless versions of the adults. This period of their development lasts through nine moults before the insects become fully adult.

Distribution and Habitat • Found in warmer areas throughout the North Island and in the northern parts of the South Island, often near buildings and in adjoining cultivated areas. The Black Field Cricket is fairly undemanding about where it chooses to live and is frequently found in such places as under fallen logs, under rocks, and in stone walls. Although it can fly, it usually prefers to scuttle off into a recess if disturbed.

Adult body length • 20 mm.

Remarks • The Black Field Cricket is another insect that often 'sings' in the evening of late summer and early autumn, filling the air with its incessant and shrill chirps. This is the insect's mating call, which it produces by rubbing its hindwings against a specialised, comb-like structure on the hindwings. The loudest singers are those preferred by the females.

The Black Field Cricket can be a serious pasture pest, especially after periods of prolonged drought, when it often reaches plague proportions. During these periods it has even been known to invade houses and devour anything even remotely edible, such as leather and wallpaper.

Adult male Black Field Cricket.

16 Katydid/Kikipounamu
Caedicia simplex

Order: ORTHOPTERA
Family: TETTIGONIIDAE

Appearance • A typical grasshopper in appearance but, unlike related species, the Katydid is uniformly green in colour. As with all Orthoptera, the hindlegs are greatly enlarged. The wings are broad and held tent-like over the body when the insect is resting. The antennae are very long and hair-like.

Development • Eggs are black and wedge-shaped, deposited on plants from about March to May with the resultant wingless nymphs being found throughout the year.

Distribution and Habitat • Widespread throughout mainland New Zealand in warmer areas. Anyone who wanders in gardens and in country areas on quiet summer nights will be familiar with the quiet, rather hesitant and staccato zip-zip song of the Katydid. The insect makes this sound by rubbing its wings together. This sound also gives the Katydid one of its alternative names, the Scissor-snip. They live mainly on shrubs and trees, but their cryptic colouration often makes them hard to see. Often, it is only their calls that give them away.

Adult body length • 40 mm.

Remarks • The Kaytydid's cryptic, leaf-like outline camouflages it rather well and even if disturbed it only moves off rather reluctantly.

It feeds on vegetation and spends a great deal of time grooming itself, rather like a cat.

The Katydid is also found in Australia.

Adult Katydid.

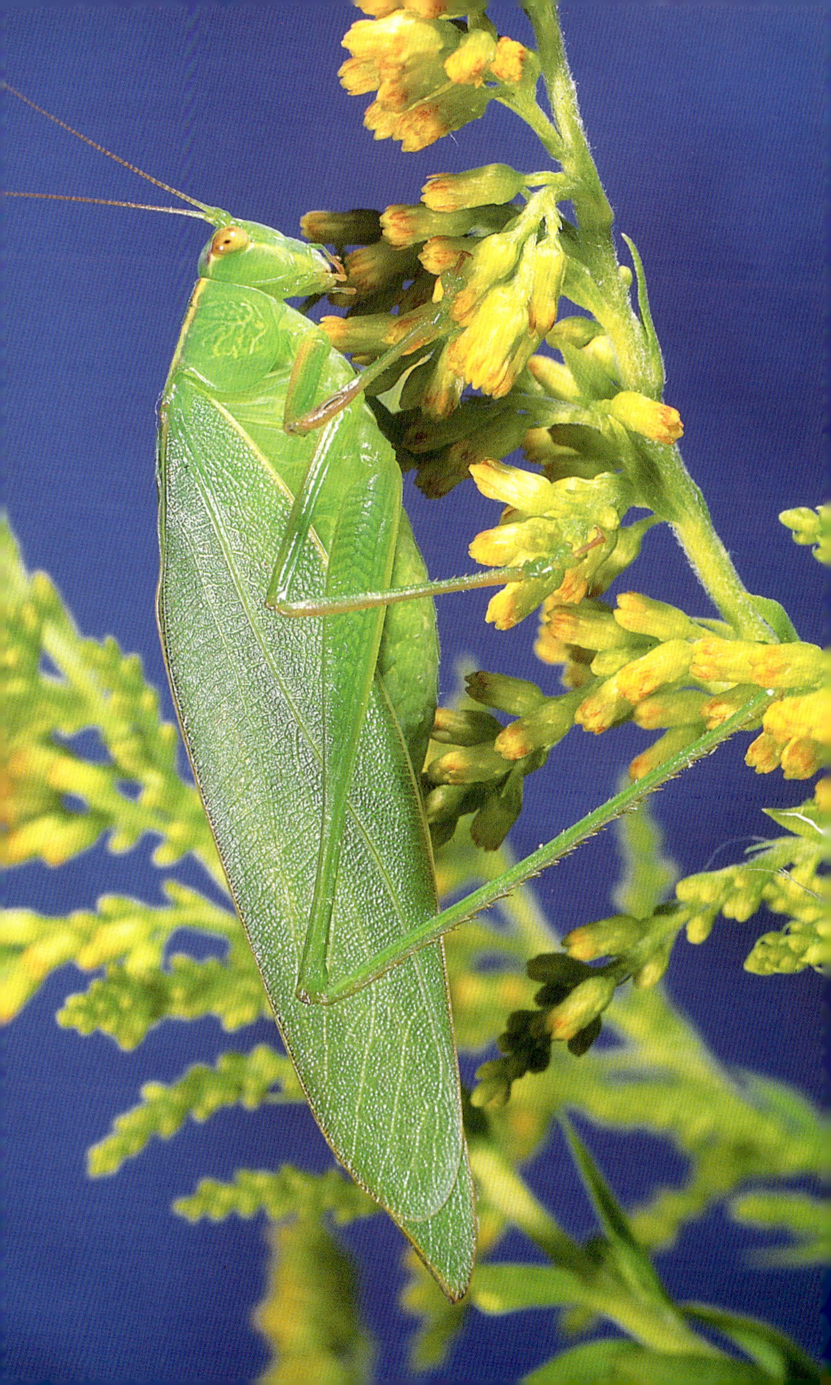

17 Migratory Locust/Kapakapa
Locusta migratoria
Order: ORTHOPTERA
Family: ACRIDIDAE

Appearance • A medium-sized, rather drab, dark-brown insect with prominent compound eyes and wings which extend the length of the body and large hindlegs.

Development • The females lay their eggs in the ground in the autumn. The eggs hatch out as nymphs in the spring and are smaller, wingless versions of the adults. After a series of moults they eventually mature as fully developed and winged adults.

Distribution and Habitat • The Migratory Locust is one of the most widespread of all insects. The species that is found in New Zealand is also found as far afield as Asia and Africa. Migratory Locusts are widespread throughout the North Island and the top half of the South Island as far south as mid-Canterbury, in rough pasture, secondary growth and natural grasslands, although mostly at lower altitudes.

Adult body length • 50 mm.

Remarks • Locusts in New Zealand lead somewhat of a different lifestyle to their cousins overseas. Overseas, these insects spend much of their lives as solitary individuals but at certain times, and in certain conditions, they come together in vast numbers called plagues and devastate crops, sometimes causing famine. Fortunately, in New Zealand, they never swarm.

Locusts are entirely vegetarian.

Prickly Stick Insect/Ro

Order: PHASMATODEA *Acanthoxyla prasina* **18**

Family: PHASMATIDAE

Appearance • Long, slow-moving, stick-like, drab-coloured insect which is well-camouflaged by the branches in which it shelters. It has no wings, a small head, a long thorax and abdomen, and proportionately very long legs. It is very difficult to spot unless it moves.

Development • Mating takes up a fair amount of time for most insects. Stick insects are interesting in that they have done away with this activity. The females reproduce without fertilisation, a procedure called parthenogenesis. As a result of this, all baby stick insects share identical genes to their mothers. This means that their ability to adapt to changes in their environment is very limited, making them vulnerable to such things as diseases. The female scatters her eggs at random and the emergent juveniles are miniature versions of the adults.

Distribution and Habitat • Stick Insects, sometimes called Walking Sticks, are not uncommon in New Zealand, with about 30 species occurring here. They belong to the insect order Phasmatodea, which means 'ghost-like'. The Prickly Stick Insect, unlike some related species, is flightless. When disturbed it usually freezes, hoping that it will go unnoticed. This usually works as the insect is fairly difficult to spot. It spends much of its time in its host trees, mostly manuka, kanuka and rata, where it browses on the leaves. It is widespread throughout mainland New Zealand, wherever its host trees are found.

Adult body length • 110 mm.

Female Stick Insect laying eggs.

19 Backswimmer/Hoe Tuara
Anisops assimilis

Order: HEMIPTERA
Family: NOTONECTIDAE

Appearance • A small, brownish insect that swims upside-down. The eyes are prominent and the long hindlegs have obvious hairy fringes. The Backswimmer regularly replenishes its air supply from the water's surface. An air bubble is trapped on the Backswimmer's abdomen, giving it a silvery appearance.

Development • The Backswimmer is a fast-swimming predator and is insectivorous, preying on mosquito larvae, midges and even cannibalising the nymphs of its own species. It attacks its prey from below and has a stout, sucking beak with which it sucks out the body fluids of its prey. It can also give quite a sharp jab if provoked. Eggs are laid in the tissues of aquatic plants. After laying, the adults often hibernate in the mud at the bottom of ponds.

Distribution and Habitat • Backswimmers are widespread throughout mainland New Zealand, from North Cape to Stewart Island. They are found in just about any suitable habitat — saline coastal pools, ponds, lakes, water tanks and in the slower areas of streams from coastal areas up into montane and alpine areas. They often congregate in large numbers in the shelter of vegetation overhanging water.

Adult body length • 8 mm.

Remarks • At certain times of the year Backswimmers take to the wing and migrate in large swarms.

Backswimmers are a popular food item for trout and New Zealand's native Galaxiid fishes.

Another common Backswimmer is *Anisops wakefieldi*, which largely replaces *A. assimilis* in the South Island and on Stewart Island.

Adult Backswimmer.

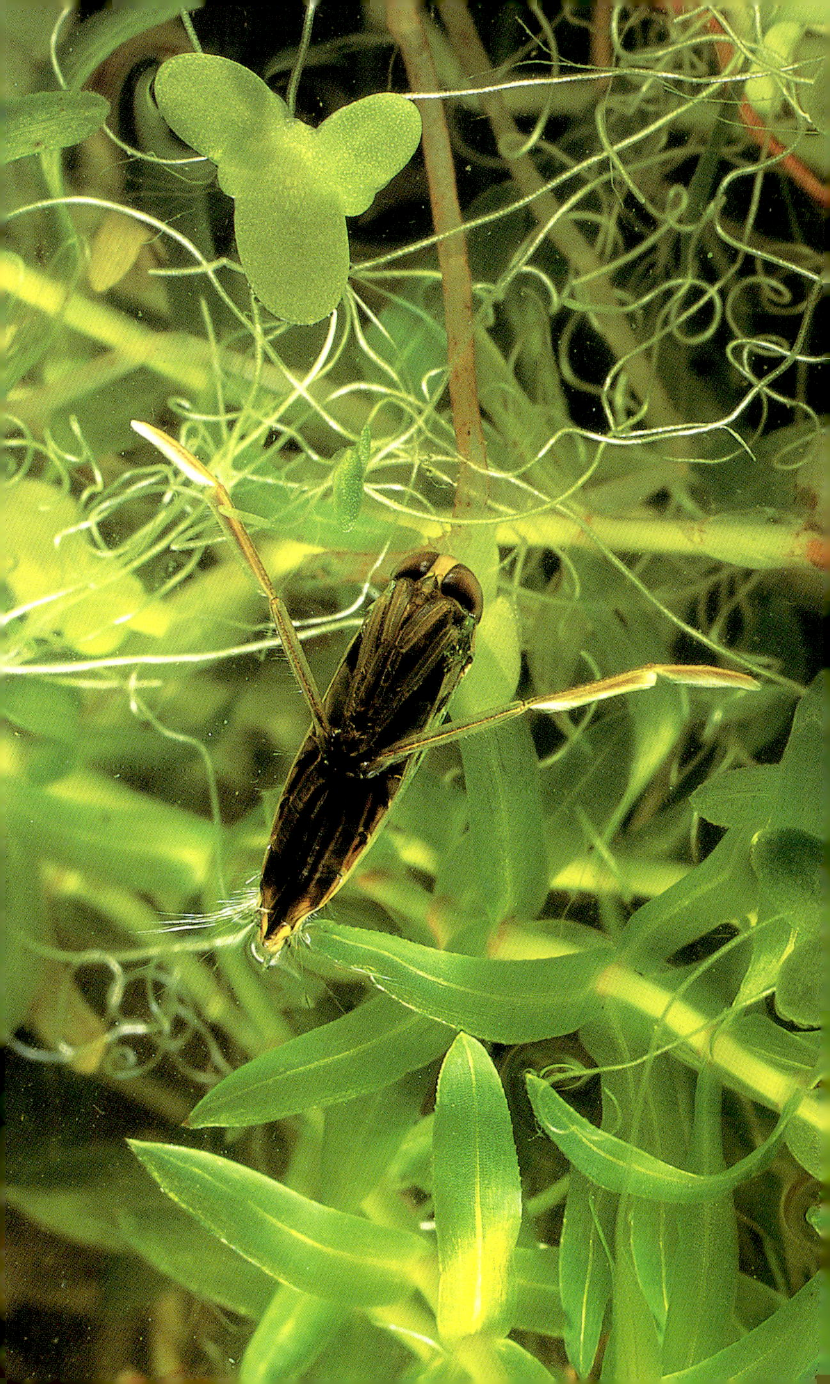

Clapping Cicada/Kihikihi Wawa
20 *Amphipsalta cingulata*

Order: HEMIPTERA
Family: CICADIDAE

Appearance • A fairly large insect with a black abdomen banded with brown and with a greenish thorax. The wings are large and transparent. It has prominent compound eyes with three simple eyes, which are known as ocelli, between them.

Development • Female cicadas lay eggs on the leaves of their host trees. The newly hatched nymphs drop to the ground where they live underground for several years before their final moult when they emerge as adults. The empty nymph cases are a familiar sight on fences, posts and tree trunks.

Distribution and Habitat • Clapping Cicadas are widespread throughout New Zealand and are found in a variety of habitats ranging from scrub to pastureland. They do a certain amount of damage to plants by sucking their juices and depositing eggs inside the plants' tissue. The Clapping Cicada first arrived in New Zealand in the 1940s, when it was noticed in New Plymouth. It is now well established throughout the North Island and the top half of the South Island. It has become a serious pest to horticulture.

Adult body length • 30 mm.

Remarks • On hot summer days the massed chorus of thousands of cicadas is almost overpowering. However, their noise is recognised as an indication that summer has well and truly arrived.

The charming Maori name translates as 'roaring like heavy rain', and is certainly most descriptive.

We have many native species of cicada, often erroneously called locusts. All have their own distinctive song.

Above: Adult Clapping Cicada.

Right: Clapping Cicada nymph emerging from underground chamber.

Below: Case of recently emerged Clapping Cicada adult.

21 Cabbage Aphid
Brevicoryne brassicae

Order: HEMIPTERA
Family: APHIDIDAE

Appearance • A minute, stout and soft-bodied little insect with spindly legs and long straight antennae. The Cabbage Aphid ranges in colour from brown to green. Two dark, horn-like projections are carried towards the rear of the abdomen.

Development • The Cabbage Aphid is, like the Prickly Stick Insect, parthenogenetic, in that it can reproduce without mating. It gives birth to live young, which are continually produced throughout the year. The young are miniature versions of the adults, increasing in size with each moult.

Distribution and Habitat • Widespread throughout mainland New Zealand wherever host plants occur.

Adult body length • 2 mm.

Remarks • Cabbage Aphids are among the numerous pests that migrated along with European colonists to New Zealand. They are also among the most familiar of pests to the home gardener, damaging plants by sucking their juices.

As its scientific name suggests, this aphid specialises in vegetables of the *Brassica* group, which includes plants such as cabbages and cauliflowers. Cabbage Aphids are, like Passionvine Hoppers, vectors, or carriers, of a number of harmful plant viruses.

Although Cabbage Aphids sometimes live alone, more often they congregate in colonies. It is in these aggregations that they do the most damage.

Other aphid species have different host plants. These range from oaks and elms to legumes and potatoes.

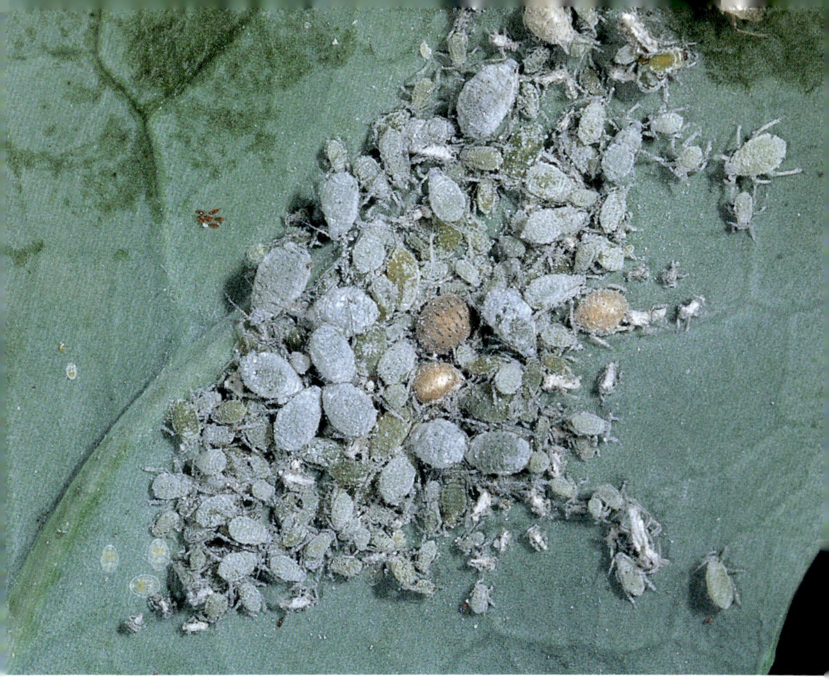

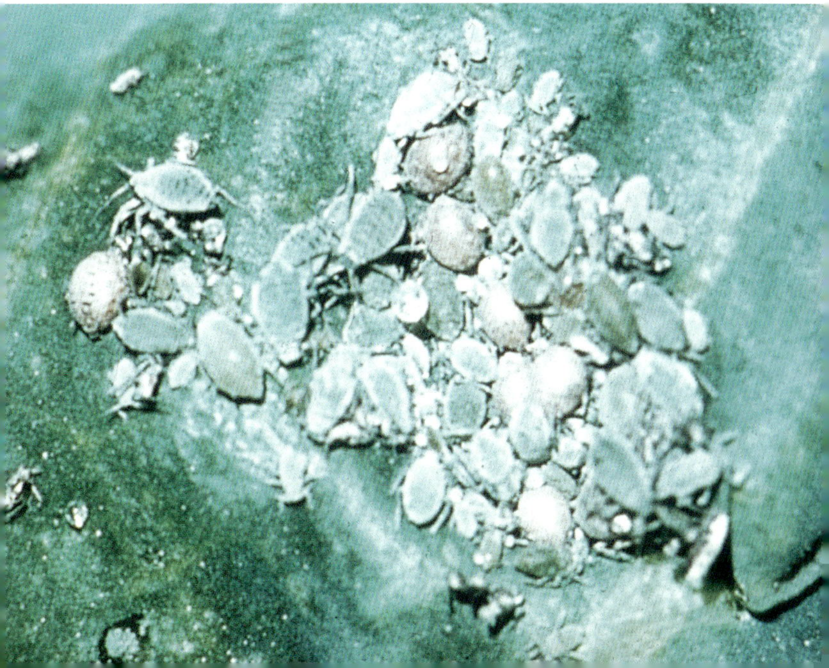

22 Green Vegetable Bug/Kiri Wenua Kakariki
Nezara viridula

Order: HEMIPTERA
Family: PENTATOMIDAE

Appearance • A small, squat, shield-shaped insect whose antennae are half the length of its body.

Development • A very prolific insect that lays clusters of barrel-shaped eggs on the underside of leaves at regular intervals throughout the year. Immature Green Vegetable Bugs are similar in shape to the adults, but are considerably smaller and are blackish in colour.

Distribution and Habitat • Widespread throughout the North Island as well as in Nelson and Marlborough, in the South Island.

Adult body length • 15 mm.

Remarks • Like other horticultural pests, the Green Vegetable Bug damages plants by sucking the juices of its host plant.

When agitated, the Green Vegetable Bug emits a foul-smelling secretion that seems to deter predatory birds, but this is not so effective against other insects. However, an introduced Egyptian egg parasite, *Microphanturus basalis*, is a major predator of the Green Vegetable Bug early in its breeding season.

This bug is unusual in that it uses sound for sexual communication. Researchers have found that the male stridulates, producing up to seven distinct songs. Females produce three.

ABOVE: Adult Green Vegetable Bug on hatching egg cluster.

LEFT: Mating pairs of Green Vegetable Bug.

BELOW: Green Vegetable Bug nymphs.

23 Passionvine Hopper
Scolypopa australis

Order: HEMIPTERA
Family: RICANIIDAE

Appearance • A small, dark-coloured bug with large wings that are held tent-like over the body. These wings are mostly transparent but have some black blotches and lines.

Development • The nymphs of the Passionvine Hopper, which emerge each spring, are tiny, drab, wingless hoppers, with distinctive white tufts at the end of their abdomens. They are a favoured prey of ichneumonid wasps.

Distribution and Habitat • The Passionvine Hopper arrived in New Zealand from Australia late last century. It is now a common garden pest throughout much of the North Island as well as in the northern areas of the South Island.

Adult body length • 10 mm.

Remarks • Surprisingly, the Passionvine Hopper is quite a rare insect in its native Australia, presumably because in Australia there is a predatory insect that acts as a natural biological control.

The Passionvine Hopper damages plants by puncturing them, and then sucking up the juices that ooze from them. This is then secreted by the insect as a sweet, sticky substance called honeydew, which is often harvested by Honey Bees.

In some areas the Passionvine Hopper will utilise the native plant tutu, *Coriaria sarmentosa*, as a food source. As the tutu is highly poisonous, so is the resultant honeydew. This toxin consequently carries through to the honey that bees produce from the honeydew. Because of this, honey production is banned at certain times of the year in some areas where tutu is common.

The virus that started devastating cabbage trees, *Cordyline* spp., in many parts of New Zealand in the late 1980s is apparently being spread by this insect.

Adult Passionvine Hopper.

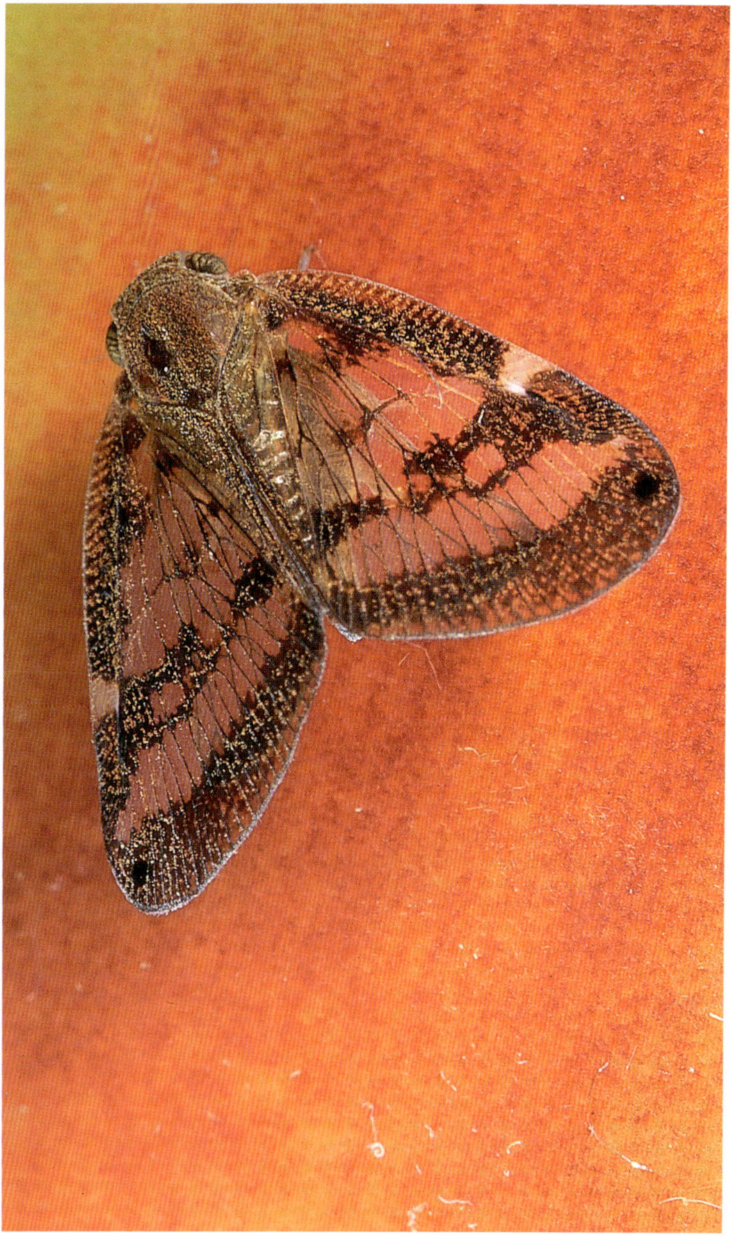

24 Watermeasurer
Hydrometra risbeci

Order: HEMIPTERA
Family: HYDROMETRIDAE

Appearance • The antennae of the Watermeasurer are roughly half the length of the insect's body. The elongated, thin, middle and hind legs are used to skate on the surface of water. The head is also very elongated. The insect varies between straw-brown and dark-brown in colour.

Development • A number of narrow, seed-like eggs are laid just above the water surface on vegetation. The eggs are attached by short stalks. The emergent larvae are smaller, wingless versions of the adult Watermeasurer.

Distribution and Habitat • Watermeasurers are widespread in still waters throughout the North Island. There is a closely related, but as yet unnamed, species found in thermal areas.

Adult body length • 14 mm.

Remarks • Although capable of quite a turn of speed when necessary, Watermeasurers usually pick their way across the surface of the water in a fairly leisurely fashion. In fact, it is so leisurely that these insects are quite hard to spot.

Watermeasurers are carnivorous, or to be exact, they are insectivorous. Although they take many of their prey from the water's surface, sometimes they also search out their victims completely submerged under the water. Mosquito larvae make up most of the Watermeasurer's diet but other insects are also occasionally taken. The Watermeasurer seizes these larvae and sucks out their body fluids.

The Watermeasurer ripples the water surface to communicate with others of the species.

In a given population, some insects will be flighted and some will be flightless.

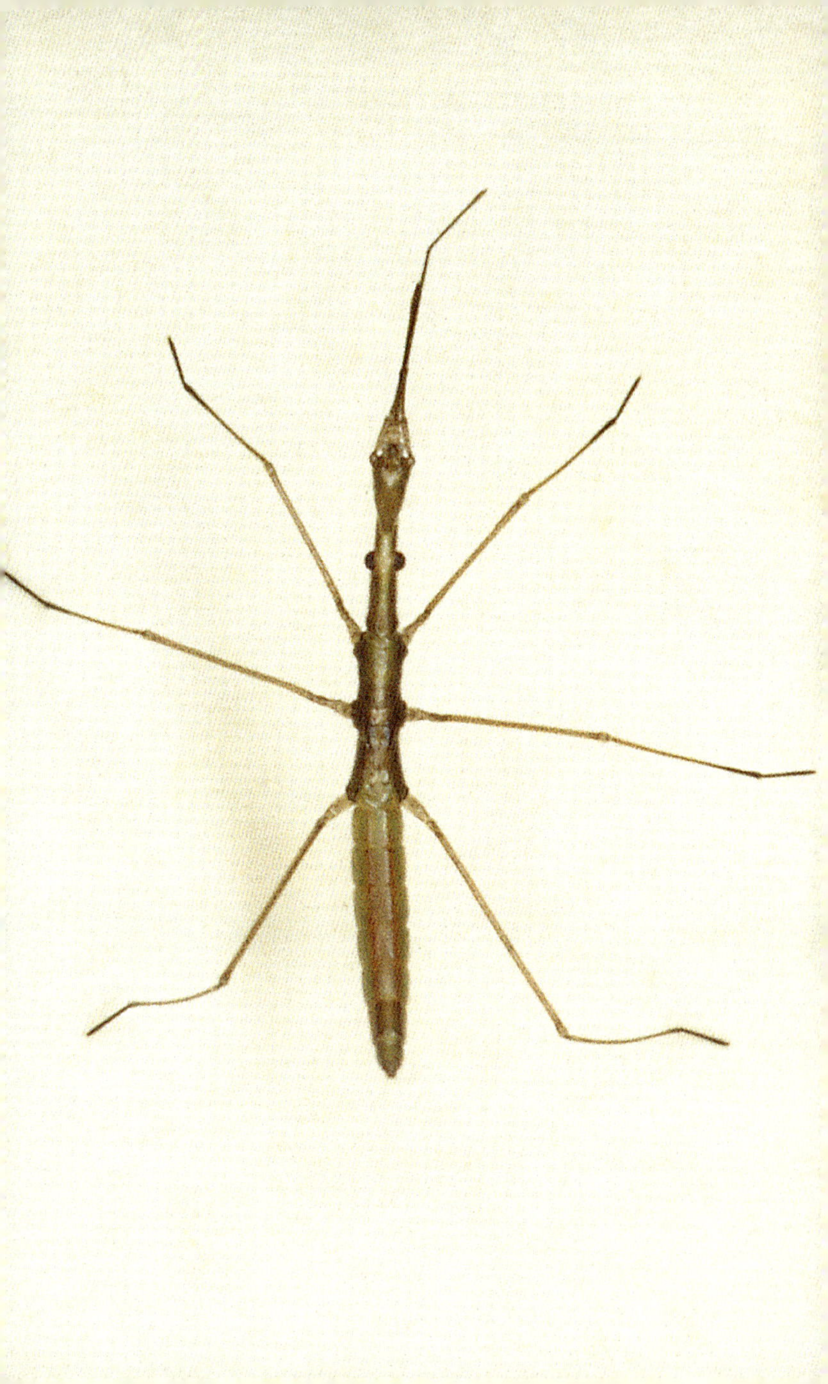

25 Waterboatman/Hoehoe Tuara
Sigara arguta

Order: HEMIPTERA
Family: CORIXIDAE

Appearance • A small, dark-coloured aquatic insect which, unlike the Backswimmer, swims the right way up, using the middle and hind legs for propulsion.

Development • Waterboatmen lay their eggs on aquatic vegetation.

Distribution and Habitat • Waterboatmen are found in ponds and the more sheltered waters of lakes and even sometimes in the slower waters of some streams. Waterboatmen are surprisingly good fliers, migrating between ponds when necessary.

Adult body length • 5 mm.

Remarks • This insect is vegetarian, feeding on microscopic algae and detritus at the bottom of ponds. Because of this they are usually only seen when they return to the surface for air. This air they carry with them as a bubble, which is transported among the hairs on their slightly concave abdomens.

Waterboatmen propel themselves along with their strong hind legs, using their middle legs to anchor themselves to the bottom, or to aquatic vegetation, while they are feeding.

A rather similar Waterboatman, *Diaprepocoris zealandica*, is more common in weedier habitats.

Adult Waterboatman.

Greenhouse Thrip

Order: THYSANOPTERA *Heliothrips haemorrhoidalis*
Family: THRIPIDAE

26

Appearance • Greenhouse thrips are readily distinguished from other insects in that their wings are merely narrow strips fringed with long, stiff hairs. Although these are sufficient to propel them through the air, they are not powerful enough to get them airborne. This state they achieve by first leaping into the air, then flapping their wings.

Development • Thrips can be male, female or bisexual. The eggs are inserted into plant tissues and the new hatchlings are smaller, wingless versions of the adults. These go through four moults before maturing.

Distribution and Habitat • There are some 4500 species of thrips worldwide. Many have been accidentally introduced to New Zealand.

Adult body length • 2 mm.

Remarks • Although minute, these insects can build up to such large numbers that at times they become serious horticultural pests. They colonise plants in immense numbers, feeding on sap and eating pollen. In such large numbers they speckle their host plants with their black excrement, causing the plants to turn brown.

Greenhouse Thrips are the favoured food of the tiny crabronid wasps *Rhopalum* spp., which store them in the disused burrows of small wood borers.

27 Dobsonfly/Ngaro Parirau
Archichauliodes diversus Order: MEGALOPTERA
Family: CORYDALIDAE

Appearance • The Dobsonfly is a medium-sized insect with long, tapering antennae and four large, membranous, similarly sized wings. It is brownish in colour with the front wings being darker than the hind wings.

Development • Females lay masses of eggs on rocks emerging from the water. On hatching, the larvae drop into the water where they remain for several years, going through a series of moults. The larvae, which vaguely resemble aquatic centipedes, have been given a number of names by anglers, including the 'Black-creeper' and the 'Toe-biter'. It preys on the larvae of other aquatic insects, particularly those of the mayflies, but in turn the Dobsonfly is eaten by trout and also by some native fishes. At maturity, the larvae dig a hole into the stream banks where they over-winter, emerging as adults in the spring.

Distribution and Habitat • In streams and rivers throughout New Zealand.

Adult body length • 25 mm.

Remarks • Sometimes called the Alderfly.

The Dobsonfly is one of the largest of New Zealand's aquatic insects and is endemic to this country. The adults are poor fliers as they are large and have awkward wings.

Adult Dobsonfly.

Antlion/Kutukutu
Weeleus acutus

28

Order: NEUROPTERA
Family: MYRMELEONITIDAE

Appearance • The Antlion has a long, thin body with two pairs of wings of roughly equal size. These are flecked with brown. The larva is a small, drab, louse-like creature with a squat abdomen and a small, flattish thorax and prominent jaws.

Development • Many insects have developed their own particular strategies for capturing their prey. Among the most fascinating of these must surely be that of the Antlion. Unlike most other insects that lurk in wait for their meals to wander by, the Antlion actually constructs a trap. The female Antlion seeks out a suitable position, usually in friable soil in a sheltered area such as that afforded by banks or by trees, or even by an old building. Here an egg is laid. On hatching, the nymph burrows down into the soil, digging a cone-shaped pit. It then waits in the centre of the pit with just its jaws exposed. Insects, spiders and slaters wandering by fall into the trap and slide to their doom. Often the Antlion helps things along by bombarding the struggling victim with carefully aimed particles of dirt. After several months the larva spins itself a globular silken cocoon and pupates, eventually emerging as the elegant lace-winged adult.

Distribution and Habitat • Widespread but somewhat sporadic distribution throughout the country, from lowland to montane areas.

Adult body length: 30 mm.

Winged adult Antlion.

29 Carabid Beetle/Kurikuri
Megadromus capito

Order: COLEOPTERA
Family: CARABIDAE

Appearance • A medium-sized, flattish beetle, with long legs, a striated carapace and prominent jaws. It is dark brown to black in colour and the head is narrower than the thorax, which is in turn narrower than the abdomen.

Development • Eggs are laid in rotting logs and the larvae go through several stages, or 'instars', before emerging as adults. During these juvenile stages, the mother Carabid Beetle remains with the young.

Distribution and Habitat • Carabid Beetles are a conspicuous element of our insect fauna with many species found in New Zealand. A good percentage of these are endemic, many of which are endangered. During the day they are frequently found in rotting wood and their successful adaptation to their ground-dwelling environment means that many have completely lost all traces of their wings.

Adult body length • 25 mm.

Remarks • A closely related species to the Carabid Beetle is the Ground Beetle, *Megadromus vigil*, an attractive shiny, bluish-black beetle common in the Wellington area. Another common species is *Placomostethus planiusculus*.

Carabid Beetles are sometimes also called Ground Beetles. Like many of their close relatives they are predacious, with a number also having carnivorous larvae. Although their prey are usually small invertebrates, the beetles should be handled with some care because their sharp pincer-like mandibles have been known to give quite a painful nip.

Carabid Beetles spend their days under rotting logs and prowl around the forest floor at night in search of their prey.

Adult Carabid Beetle.

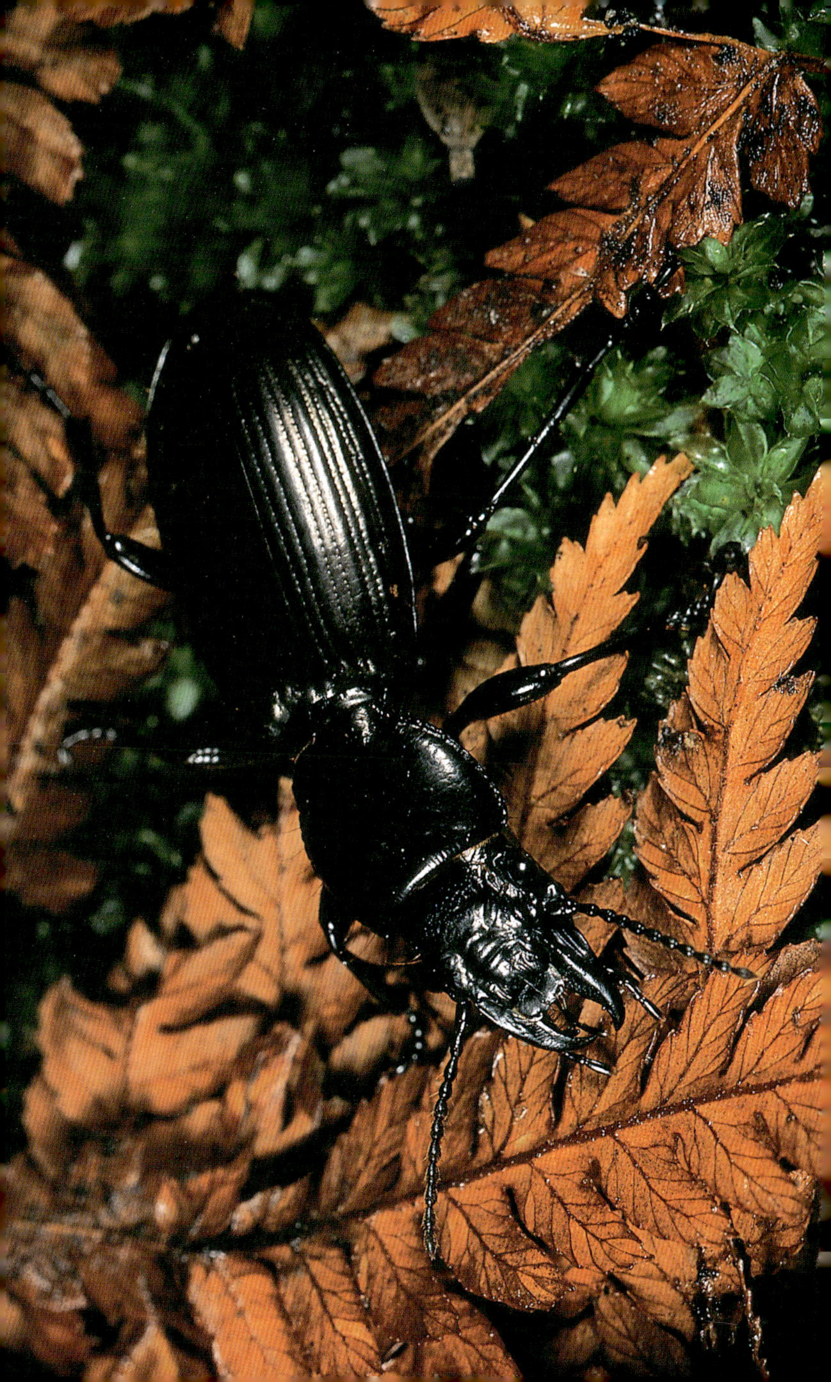

30 Cosmopolitan Diving Beetle/Wai Tataka
Rhantus pulverosus

Order: COLEOPTERA
Family: DYTISCIDAE

Appearance • Heavily sclerotised forewings. Antennae usually not visible. Swims rapidly below the surface with a somewhat jerky movement, using its long, densely fringed hindlegs for propulsion.

Development • The larva of this beetle is as voracious a predator as the adult, unhesitatingly tackling prey much larger than itself. Because of this habit, anglers call it the 'Water Tiger'. The larvae either swim about or crawl over the bottom sediment of areas of shallow, still water such as ponds and lake edges, searching for aquatic insects which they seize with their pincer-like jaws. However, as they lack gills, they need to rise to the water surface to breathe.

Distribution and Habitat • Many different kinds of aquatic beetle inhabit just about any sizable patch of still water throughout the country, but the Cosmopolitan Diving Beetle is the best known, and probably the most widespread of these. It is found in many countries, just about worldwide, which is where the name Cosmopolitan comes from.

Adult body length • 15 mm.

Remarks • This beetle propels itself rapidly through the water by the use of its strong hind legs, constantly searching out its prey, which ranges in size from the minute larvae of other aquatic insects up to fish several times its own size.

When the Cosmopolitan Diving Beetle needs to replenish its air supply, it thrusts the tip of its wing cases through the water surface, taking in a bubble of air.

Sometimes also called Whirligig Beetle, although the true Whirligig Beetle is a recently arrived species from Australia, *Gyrinus convexiusculus*, which is now established in the Waikato region and belongs to another family, the Gyrinidae.

Other commonly encountered Dytiscidae diving beetles are *Berosus pallidipennis*, which lives in stony streams in both islands; *Limnoxenus zealandicus*, which commonly frequents weed-choked ponds; and a seemingly undescribed *Paracymus* sp., which frequents North Island thermal pools.

Adult Diving Beetle.

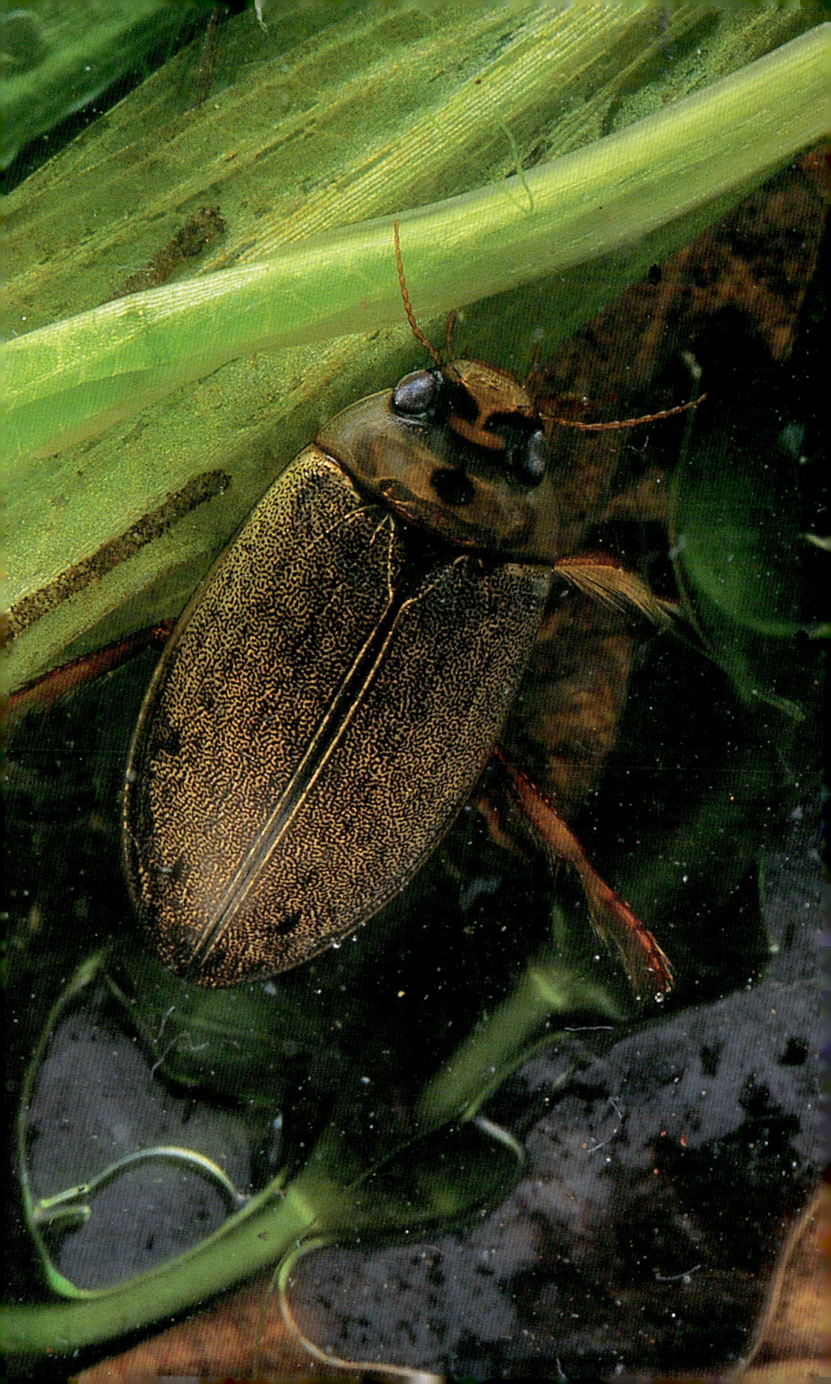

31 Devil's Coachhorse Beetle
Creophilus oculatus

Order: COLEOPTERA
Family: STAPHYLINIDAE

Appearance • Medium-sized, elongated, dark beetle with conspicuous orange spots behind eyes. Curls abdomen and opens jaws when threatened.

Development • Both the adults and larvae are predators, with the adults often preying on flies' maggots, which they first tear apart and then suck out their juices.

Distribution and Habitat • Introduced from Europe and now widespread near inhabited areas throughout mainland New Zealand.

Adult body length • 20 mm.

Remarks • The Devil's Coachhorse Beetle was held in some awe in medieval Europe, where it was thought to be a devil which 'eats the bodies of sinners'. This was because this beetle is commonly found in carcasses.

When disturbed or harassed, this beetle produces a rather nasty secretion from its abdominal glands, which smells like rotten fish.

The Devil's Coachhorse Beetle is also found in Australia.

Adult Devil's Coachhorse Beetle.

Order: COLEOPTERA
Family: CARIBIDAE

Tiger Beetle/Kui
Neocicindela tuberculata   32

Appearance • Distinctively marked and smallish. A nervously active beetle with large eyes and prominent biting mouthparts. Has long legs well-adapted for running.

Development • In late spring the female drills many holes in suitable ground and lays an egg in each hole. The newly hatched larva spend the next couple of years living in this tunnel with just its head exposed, waiting for an unwary insect to wander by. The tunnel is enlarged as the larva grows. Each winter it plugs up the tunnel and hibernates.

Distribution and Habitat • There are twelve endemic species of Tiger Beetle in New Zealand, this one probably the most spectacular. It is widespread throughout the North Island, wherever it can find suitable habitat. This is mostly in light scrub or on exposed ground on the edge of bush. On hot summer days it can often be seen scurrying back and forth in search of insect prey.

Adult body length • 10 mm.

Remarks • Children once fished these larvae (often called 'Butcher boys' or 'Penny doctors') out of their tunnels with pieces of straw, which the larvae would seize on to.

Adult Tiger Beetle; larva in hole.

Manuka Beetle/Kekerewai
33 *Pyronota festiva*

Order: COLEOPTERA
Family: SCARABAEIDAE

Appearance • A small, stocky beetle which occurs in a range of colours including green and brown. The sections at the end of the antennae are often held open, like a fan.

Development • Manuka Beetle larvae live underground, where they feed on the roots of grasses. They bear a close resemblance to the pasture pest, the grass grub. They emerge as adult Manuka Beetles in the spring.

Distribution and Habitat • Widespread in suitable habitat throughout the country during summer months. Commonly encountered near the manuka and kanuka flowers on which it feeds.

Adult body length • 8 mm.

Remarks • Maori baked the Manuka Beetle with the pollen of the native bulrush to make a kind of bread.

This insect often falls into streams, where it is eaten by trout.

Adult Manuka Chafer Beetle.

Huhu Beetle/Pepe Tunga

Order: COLEOPTERA
Family: CERAMBYCIDAE

Prionoplus reticularis

34

Appearance • A fairly large, oblong beetle with antennae almost the length of its body. It is brown in colour with the hard wing cases having an embossed pattern, rather like the skin of a lizard.

Development • The female Huhu Beetle lays her eggs under the bark of both exotic and native trees. The emergent larvae take up to three years to complete their life cycle of tunnelling through dead and rotting wood. These larvae, called huhu grubs, were considered a delicacy by Maori. The adult Huhu Beetles live only about two weeks and during this period they do not feed.

Distribution and Habitat • Widespread in forested areas throughout New Zealand, but more common in lowland areas.

Adult body length • 50 mm.

Adult Huhu Beetle. INSET: Huhu Beetle larva.

35 Click Beetle/Tupanapana
Conoderus exsul

Order: COLEOPTERA
Family: ELATERIDAE

Appearance • A medium-sized, black, elongated beetle, with conspicuous striations on its carapace. Its head is loosely hinged to its body.

Development • The larvae are long and cylindrical with a hardened, shiny body and are called wireworms. As they eat the roots of plants in some areas they are regarded as an agricutural pest.

Distribution and Habitat • Widespread throughout New Zealand from coastal to montane areas.

Adult body length • 15 mm.

Remarks • The Click Beetle is attracted to lights and commonly flies into houses on spring and summer evenings.

The name Click Beetle comes from the sound the insect makes when it tries to right itself if upside-down. This sound is produced by a lever-like mechanism on the Click Beetle's underside between its forelegs. The mechanism fits into a cavity on the middle thorax between the middle legs. When the lever is released the insect leaps and rights itself with a clicking sound, rather like that made by a ballpoint pen.

Adult Click Beetle.

Steelblue Ladybird/Mumutawa

Order: COLEOPTERA
Family: COCCINELLIDAE

Orcus chalybeus 36

Appearance • A tiny, shiny, steel-blue beetle with a rounded, convex body and a small thorax and abdomen. The antennae and legs are short and are usually hidden beneath the body.

Development • The female lays her eggs early in the spring near aphid or scale insect colonies. These insects are predated on by the ladybird larvae as soon as they hatch. The larvae are flattish, elongated and rather wrinkled creatures. At most, the larval stage lasts a few months.

Distribution and Habitat • Originally from Australia, the Steelblue Ladybird is now well established in citrus-growing areas in New Zealand. Like other ladybird species, the Steelblue Ladybird is most prevalent from about November to February, when their insect prey are at their peak in terms of abundance.

Adult body length • 5 mm.

Remarks • Both adults and larvae of the Steelblue Ladybird are beneficial as biological controls of such insect pests as aphids, mites and scale insects which are difficult to control with chemicals.

Most of New Zealand's best known ladybirds are imports. These include the European Two-spotted Ladybird, *Adalia bipunctata*, and the Eleven-spotted Ladybird, *Coccinella 11-punctata*. Also regularly seen are other Australian ladybirds such as the 18-spotted Ladybird, *Leis conformis*, and the Tasman Ladybird, *Coccinella leonina*.

37 Elephant Weevil
Rhyncodes ursus

Order: COLEOPTERA
Family: CURCULIONIDAE

Appearance • A squat, dumpy weevil with striated elytra. It is dull black and covered with patches of minute, yellowish hairs. In older adults these have sometimes been rubbed off.

Development • The larvae are legless, C-shaped, rather maggot-like creatures with well-developed jaws which are used for chewing their way through the wood of beech and rimu trees.

Distribution and Habitat • In beech, *Nothofagus* spp., forests throughout New Zealand.

Adult body length • 10–20 mm.

Remarks • Adult Elephant Weevils feed on the sap that oozes from beech trees.

Giraffe Weevil/Tuwhaipapa

Order: COLEOPTERA *Lasiorhynchus barbicornis*
Family: BRENTIDAE

38

Appearance • This weevil is difficult to mistake for any other insect with its distinctive long narrow body, long legs and extremely elongated proboscis. It is brownish-black in colour, with antennae carried at the tip of the proboscis in the male, but about midway along the proboscis in the slightly smaller female.

Development • Eggs are laid by the female Giraffe Weevil in holes she bores in the bark or wood of a variety of softwood trees. Here, the larvae bore tunnels in the wood as they feed and develop.

Distribution and Habitat • Throughout New Zealand wherever its host of softwood trees are found.

Adult body length • 80–100 mm.

Remarks • The Brentidae weevils differ from the 'true' weevils in that they have straight antennae that lack elbows.

Male Giraffe Weevil.

Cat Flea/Puruhi
39 *Ctenocephalides felis*

Order: SIPHONAPTERA
Family: PULICIDAE

Appearance • A small, laterally flattened insect. Its shape helps the insect to 'swim' through the fur of its host. The antennae are short and the eyes are vestigial. The legs are well developed, with the hind legs adapted for jumping.

Development: The flea lays several hundred eggs, either on the host or in the cat's sleeping area. The larvae feed on organic matter, with three moults or instars, emerging as an adult flea after several months. The vibration of an arriving host usually triggers the emergence of adult fleas.

Distribution and Habitat • Wherever cats are found Cat Fleas will probably also be present.

Adult body length: 5 mm.

Remarks • The Cat Flea, as the name implies, is found only on cats. The dog has its own flea, the Dog Flea, *Ctenocephalides canis*, and humans also have their own flea, the Human Flea, *Pulex irritans*. There are over 3000 species of fleas worldwide. Although those listed above are specific to one host animal, many other species will feed on more than one host animal.

Adult Cat Flea.

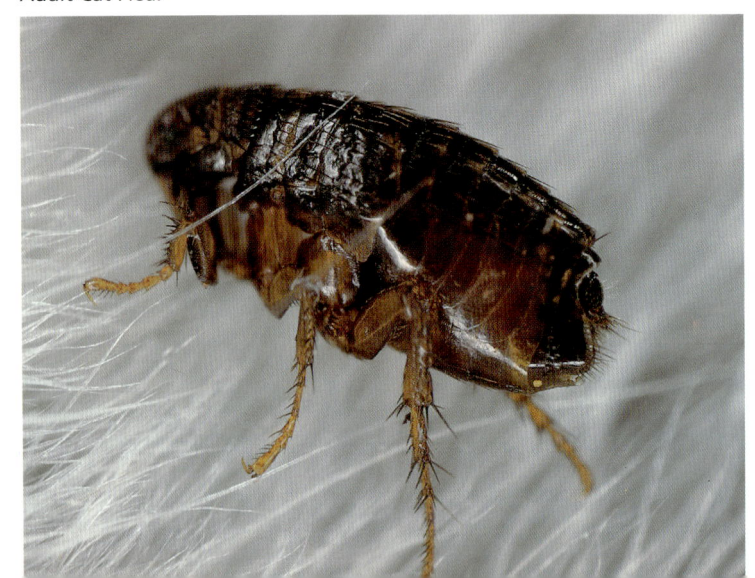

Vigilant Mosquito/Waeroa
Culex pervigilans

Order: DIPTERA
Family: CULICIDAE

40

Appearance • The antennae of the mosquito are short and feathery in the male. In the female the stiletto-like mouthparts are obvious. There is one pair of wings and the insect rests with the hind legs raised. The somewhat squat thorax is brown and the abdomen is black with white bands. The wings are generally transparent.

Development • Eggs are laid in raft-like clusters on the surface of just about any area of still water. The emergent larvae and pupae swim with a characteristic wriggle which has earned them the name 'wrigglers'. These wrigglers feed on minute microscopic detritus and tiny organisms that they extract from the water.

Distribution and Habitat • Widespread near water throughout the North and South islands from lowland to subalpine areas. Particularly prevalent around thermal areas in the South Island.

Adult body length • 5 mm.

Remarks • Only the female Vigilant Mosquito bites and the high-pitched whine it makes when flying can be intensely annoying. The male feeds only on nectar.

Breeds in the spring and summer in areas south of Auckland but from Auckland north this mosquito breeds throughout the year.

This species is replaced in some areas around Auckland as well as in Northland by another mosquito, *Culex asteliae*.

Male mosquito.

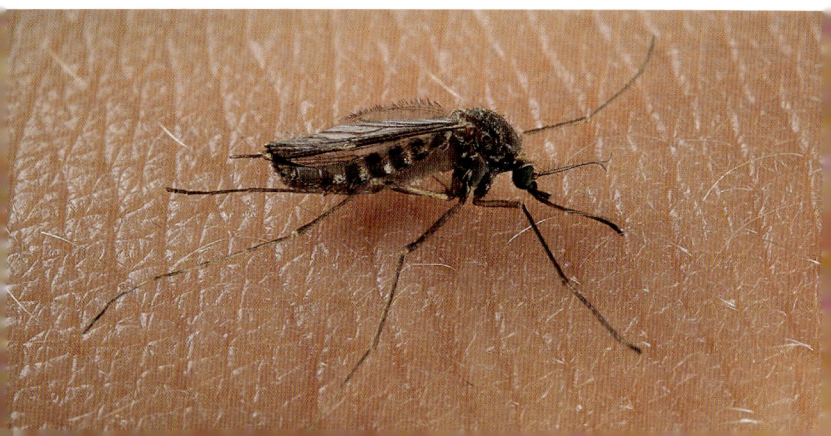

41 Sandfly/Namu
Austrosimulium australense

Order: DIPTERA
Family: SIMULIIDAE

Appearance • A tiny blackish fly with a short, squat thorax, fat abdomen and dusky wings.

Development • The female Sandfly crawls down below the water surface and deposits clumps of yellowish-orange eggs on rocks or other submerged objects. The emergent larvae cling to aquatic vegetation and rocks, feeding by filtering particles out of the water.

Distribution and Habitat • The Sandfly is found in suitable habitat such as beaches, sandy riverbanks and lake shores throughout mainland New Zealand, but is particularly plentiful to the west of the Main Divide in the South island and in Fiordland. Here, its attacks on humans have earned it a dire reputation out of all proportion to its size.

Adult body length • 2 mm.

Remarks • In parts of the South Island and on Stewart Island there is a related species, *Austrosimulium ungulatum*.

Only the female bites and this chiefly occurs on beaches, at lakesides and on riverbanks at dawn and dusk.

In other countries Sandflies are often called Black Flies.

Female Sandfly feeding on blood.

Australian Soldierfly

Order: DIPTERA
Family: STRATIOMYIDAE

Exaireta spinigera

42

Appearance • A medium-sized fly with a narrow bluish-black body. Has compound eyes and dusky wings.

Development • The Australian Soldierfly deposits its eggs in decaying vegetation such as compost, and is common in gardens in summer months.

Distribution • As its name suggests, this fly is originally from Australia. It was first seen in New Zealand early in the twentieth century, and is now found throughout the country near inhabited areas.

Adult body length • 15 mm.

Remarks • Also called the Garden Soldierfly.

A slightly larger soldierfly, the American Soldierfly, *Hermetia illucens*, first arrived here about 1942 and is now quite common in cultivated areas throughout New Zealand. Our most prevalent native soldierfly, *Odontomyia chloris*, with its broad green and black abdomen, looks much more like a blowfly and is more common in forested areas.

Adult Soldierfly.

43 Crane Fly/Matua Waeroa Rere
Holorusia novarae

Order: DIPTERA
Family: TIPULIDAE

Appearance • The body of the Crane Fly is slim and elongated and its legs are long, delicate and fall off easily. This process has been described by some authorities as 'deciduous'. The wings are smoky-grey and veined, with brown blotching.

Development • The flat, worm-like larvae are usually fairly large and brownish or greenish in colour. They are particularly prevalent buried in mud, burrowing into decaying logs, sheltering in moss or algae, or skulking among stones in marshy areas such as those found along the banks of slower streams and swamps.

Distribution and Habitat • Widespread throughout New Zealand, but commoner in lowland areas.

Adult body length • 25 mm.

Remarks • Attracted to lights, where it can sometimes occur in large numbers.

This is the largest of some 500 Tipulidae species found in New Zealand. Others that are relatively common are *Limonia nigriscens*, which lives in decaying logs along streams; *Aphrophila neozelandica*, which is common in stony streams throughout New Zealand; and *Zelandotipula fulva*, which is found from the North Island to Stewart Island.

Sometimes incorrectly called 'Daddy-long-legs'. However, the Daddy-long-legs is a spider, *Pholcus phalangioides*.

Adult Crane Fly.

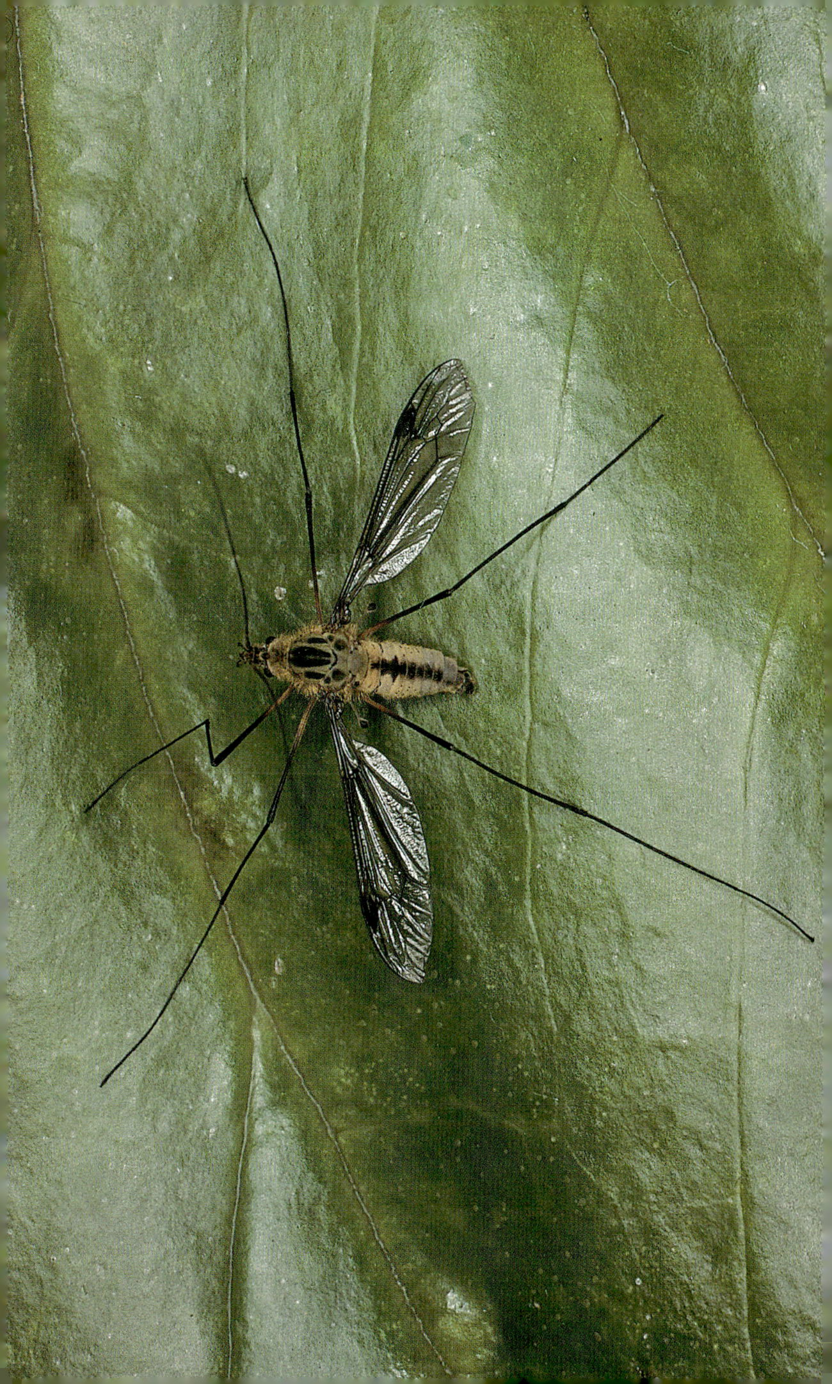

44 Golden-haired Blowfly/Rango Tuamaro
Calliphora laemica

Order: DIPTERA
Family: CALLIPHORIDAE

Appearance • A medium-sized blowfly whose abdomen is covered in patches of fine golden hairs.

Development • Eggs are deposited on putrefying objects such as dead animals. The larvae are useful in that they help dispose of carrion.

Distribution and Habitat • Widespread in the North Island, but with a more patchy distribution in the South Island.

Adult body length • 12 mm.

Remarks • Like other blowflies, the Golden-haired Blowfly is attracted into houses by the smell of food, particularly that of cooking meat.
   Makes a loud buzzing sound in flight.

Adult Blowfly.

New Zealand Blue Blowfly/Rango Pango

Order: DIPTERA *Calliphora quadrimaculata*
Family: CALLIPHORIDAE

Appearance • A medium-sized blowfly with a shiny, steel-blue abdomen, grey-black thorax and large brownish compound eyes.

Development • The eggs are deposited in dung, rotting meat or fish and decaying seaweed. Sometimes woollen materials such as blankets are targeted and 'fly-blown'.

Distribution and Habitat • Throughout mainland New Zealand but more common in lowland areas.

Adult body length • 12 mm.

Remarks • The introduced European Blue-bottle, *Calliphora erythrocephala*, is similar but its abdomen is bluish-grey in colour, less shiny and is covered in fine blackish hairs.
   The New Zealand Blue Blowfly is often attracted into houses in spring and summer, particularly when meat is being cooked.

Adult New Zealand Blue Blowfly.

46 Caddisfly/Ngaro Waiwai
Hydrobiosis parumbripennis Order: TRICHOPTERA
Family: HYDROBIOSIDAE

Appearance • A medium-sized, greenish moth-like insect with long antennae and two pairs of hairy, buff-coloured wings that are held tent-like over the body.

Development • Larvae can be divided into three groups. The first group is free-swimming, the second builds a net and the third group, to which this species belongs, builds portable cases out of twigs, small stones, shells or sand to conceal themselves from predators. They drag these cases round, like hermit crabs, until they are ready to pupate.

Distribution and Habitat • Widespread throughout New Zealand but nearly always found near water where they can sometimes be particularly abundant.

Adult body length • 20 mm.

Remarks • There are some 150 species of Caddisflies in New Zealand. Many of these have common names derived from the individual shape of the egg cases that their particular larvae construct. These include the Spiral Caddisfly, *Helicopsyche albescens*, the Net-building Caddisfly, *Hydropsyche colonica*, the Stony-cased Caddisfly, *Pycnocedtrodes aureola*, and the Horny-cased Caddisfly, *Olinga feredayi*.

Caddisflies often swarm at dawn and dusk on calm spring and summer evenings. They are readily attracted to lights and often enter houses close to streams and lakes where they flutter about.

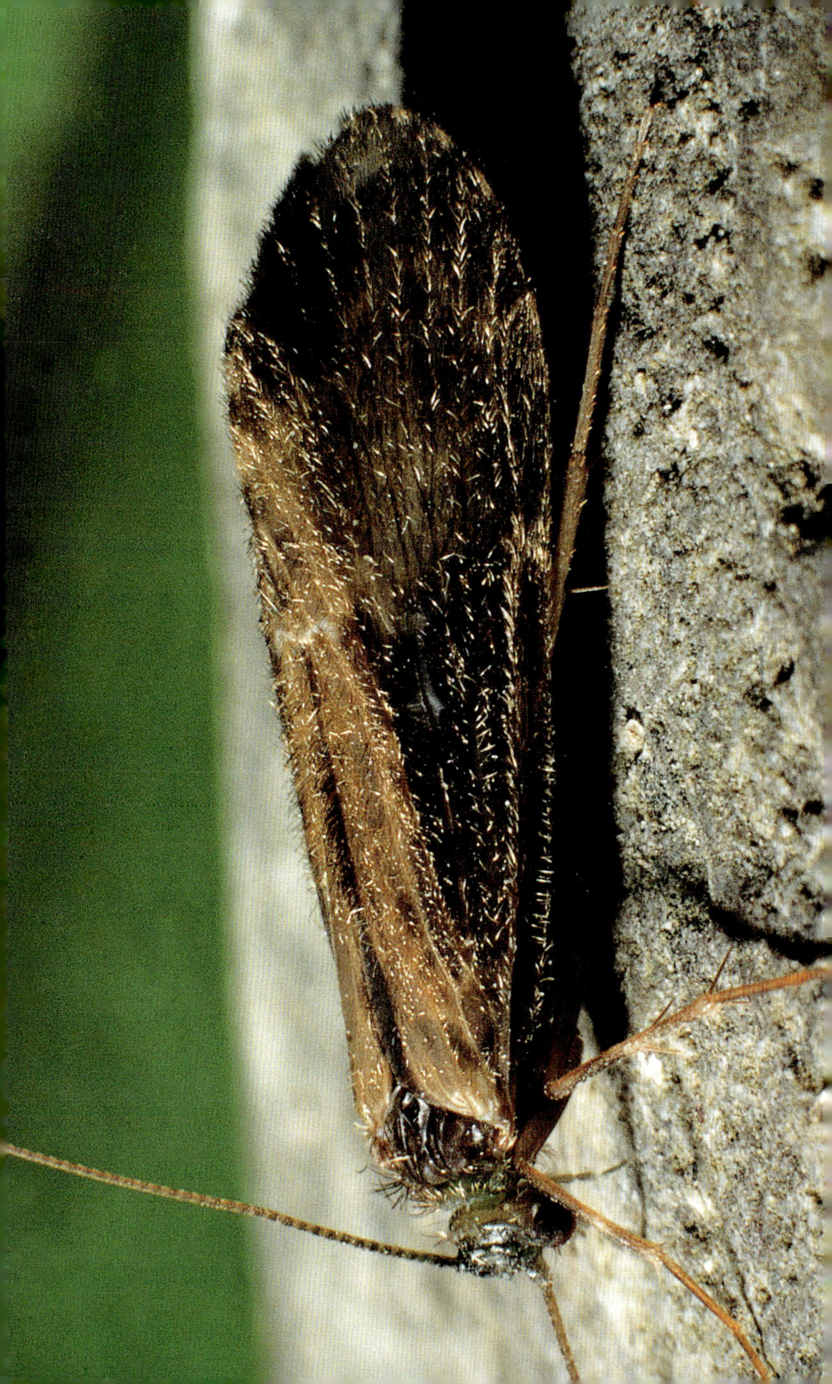

White Butterfly/Pepe Ma
47 *Pieris rapae*

Order: LEPIDOPTERA
Family: PIERIDAE

Appearance • The only white-winged butterfly in New Zealand. The forewings of the female have two black spots, while those of the male have only one.

Development • White Butterfly eggs are laid on plants of the *Brassica* group such as broccoli, cabbages and cauliflowers, on which the emergent velvety green caterpillars later feed. In turn, the caterpillars are preyed on by wasps and other species of predatory insects.

Distribution and Habitat • The White Butterfly first appeared in New Zealand in 1929, and is now widespread throughout the country, wherever their host plants, the *Brassica* group, grow. The White Butterfly is found from early spring to late autumn and there are several generations each year.

Adult wingspan • 40–50 mm.

Remarks • The White Butterfly can at times be a serious horticultural pest.

Female Cabbage White Butterfly.

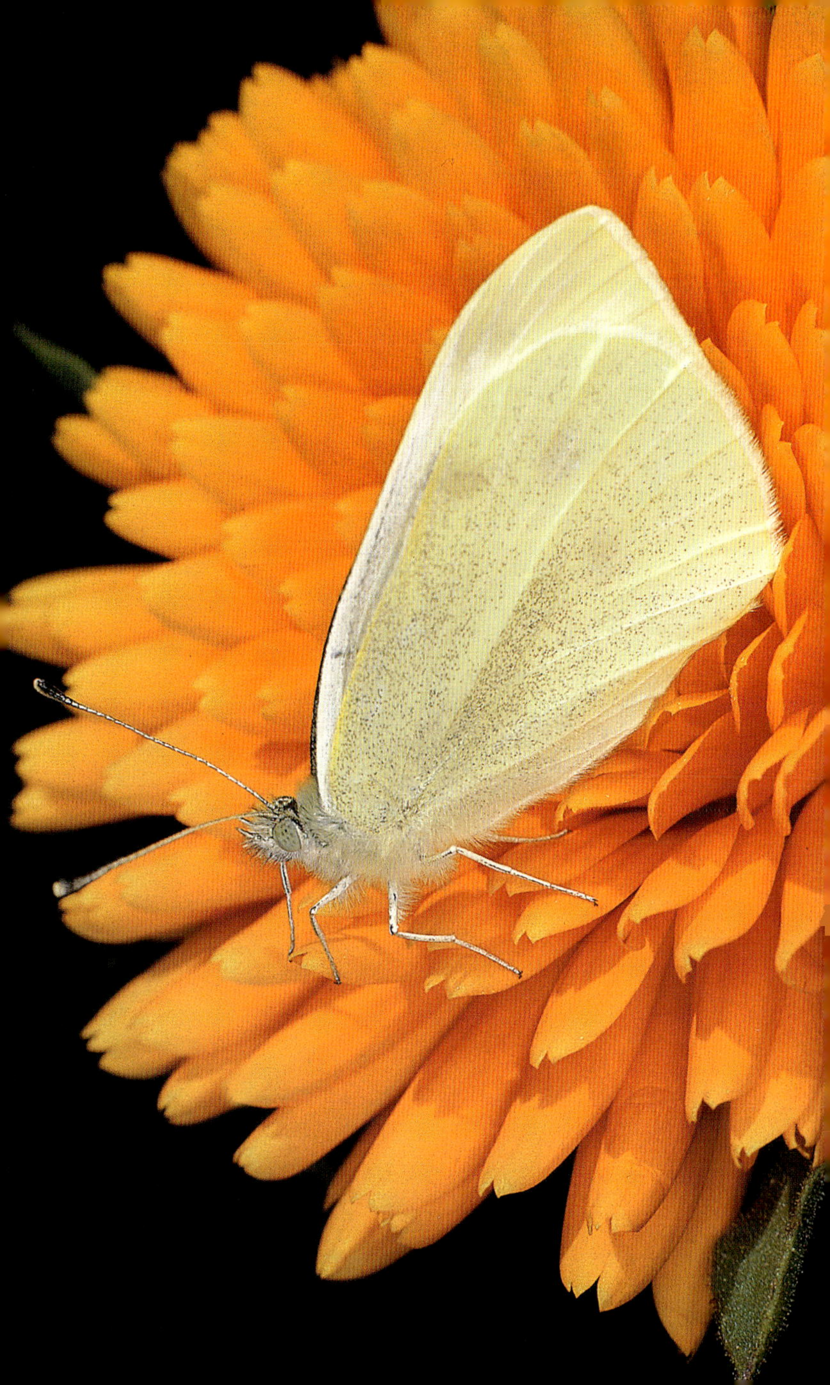

48 Monarch Butterfly/Kahuka
Danaus plexippus

Order: LEPIDOPTERA
Family: NYMPHALIDAE

Appearance • New Zealand's largest butterfly, with beautifully marked orange and black wings with white-spotted black borders. Unlikely to be mistaken for any other butterfly.

Development • The Monarch lays its eggs on the foliage of the introduced swan plant, *Asclepias physocarpa*. The emergent caterpillars go through five stages or instars before pupating and emerging as the adult Monarch.

Distribution and Habitat • Can be found throughout the year in warmer parts in the north of the country, where they cluster together in 'butterfly trees'. Occurs seasonally in the more southerly areas.

Adult wingspan • 70–100 mm.

Remarks • Once much more common. The arrival of predatory wasps in New Zealand is a major factor in their decline.

Monarch Butterflies were apparently known to the early Maori, as their Maori name, Kahuka, is one of long standing. It was only when European settlers arrived in New Zealand, bringing with them the host swan plant, that the Monarch Butterfly was able to permanently establish itself.

Newly emerged male Monarch Butterfly.

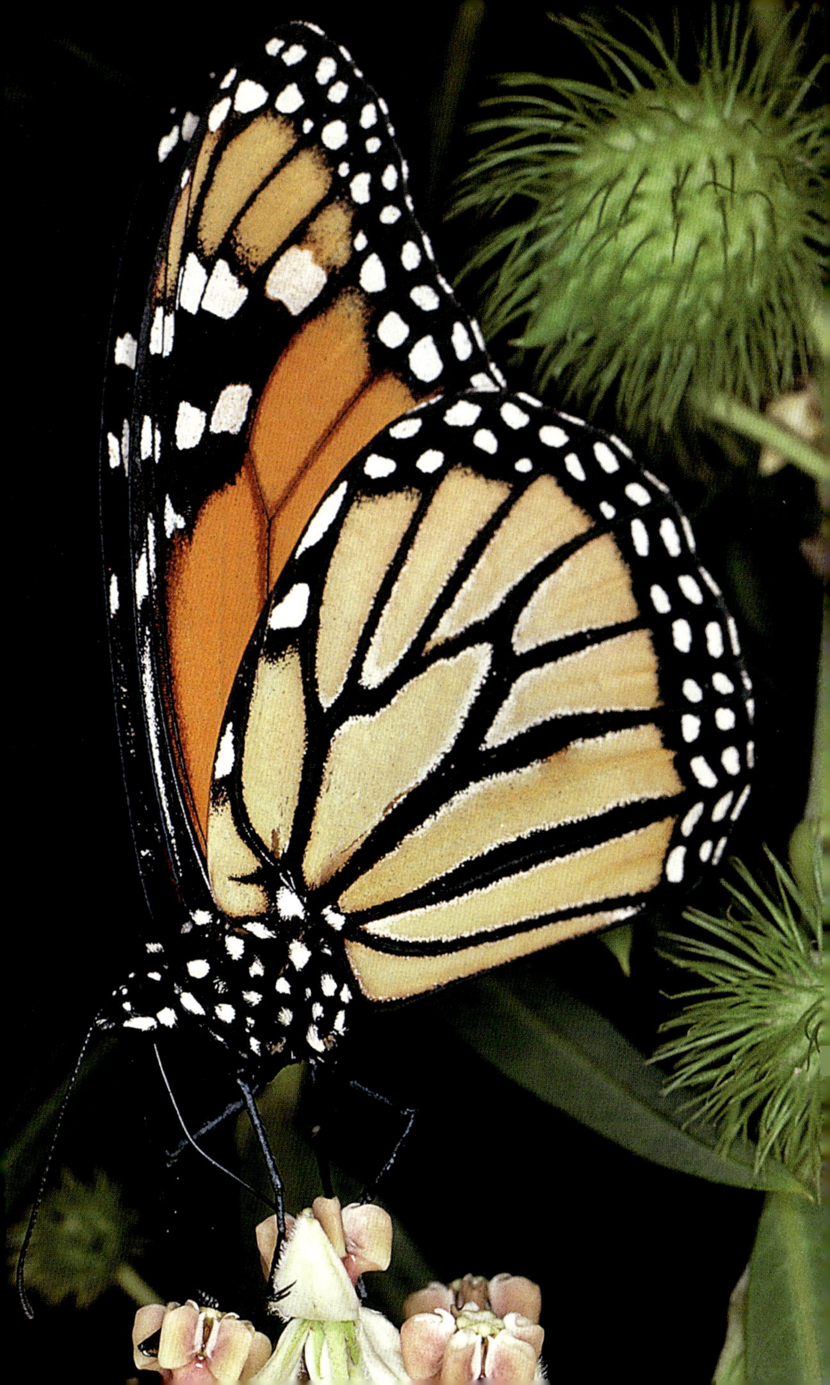

49 Common Copper/Mokarakare
Lycaena salustius

Order: LEPIDOPTERA
Family: LYCAENIDAE

Appearance • A small, jaunty, orange-brown butterfly with dark-brown stripes on its wings.

Development • Adults live for only a few days and after depositing their eggs on their host plants, various broad-leaved *Muehlenbeckia* spp., after which they die. The slug-like caterpillars are velvety-green with a conspicuous dark dorsal band. After over-wintering as a caterpillar, the Common Copper pupates and emerges as an adult butterfly in the spring.

Distribution and Habitat • The Common Copper, together with closely related species such as Rauparaha's Copper, *Lycaena rauparaha*, and the Glade Copper, *L. feredayi*, are common in coastal areas throughout New Zealand.

Adult wingspan • 25–30 mm.

Remarks • The flight of the Common Copper is strong, rapid and jerky and usually close to the ground.

Male Common Copper.

German Wasp/Wahipi
Vespula germanica

50

Order: HYMENOPTERA
Family: VESPIDAE

Appearance • Has typical wasp markings and colouration, but the face has three black dots, seen head on.

Development • A large papery nest is built, usually underground, from chewed bark and paper but occasionally they are constructed in buildings or amongst vegetation.

In winter the queen hibernates but the workers die. Like the Common Wasp, this wasp collects large numbers of insects and spiders to feed its larvae.

Distribution and Habitat • Widespread throughout New Zealand on the three main islands.

Adult body length • 22 mm.

Adult worker German Wasp.

51 Common Wasp/Wahipi
Vespula vulgaris

Order: HYMENOPTERA
Family: VESPIDAE

Appearance • Wasp markings, colouration and 'wasp-waist' typify this wasp. Separating the Common Wasp from the similar German Wasp is rather difficult, but head on, this wasp's face has a black mark on it, rather like an anchor. Also, the Common Wasp has dots and rings on the abdomen that are fused together, unlike the German Wasp, which has dots and rings that are clearly separate.

Development • The larvae are initially fed on the bodies of spiders and insects that the adults collect, but as they mature this diet switches to sugary substances such as the honeydew collected from beech trees. As with the German Wasp, a large nest with a narrow entrance is built underground out of chewed up bark and paper. This is abandoned after the larvae mature. Only the queen survives the winter by hibernating in a dark place.

Distribution and Habitat • Widespread throughout the country. Despite its name, the Common Wasp is less common than the German Wasp.

Adult body length • 22 mm.

Remarks • The name Common Wasp is rather a misnomer, as the German Wasp is more common. The German Wasp was the first to arrive in New Zealand, imported accidentally during the 1940s inside aircraft parts from Britain. The Common Wasp arrived here only in 1978, probably via Australia.

Common Wasp workers.

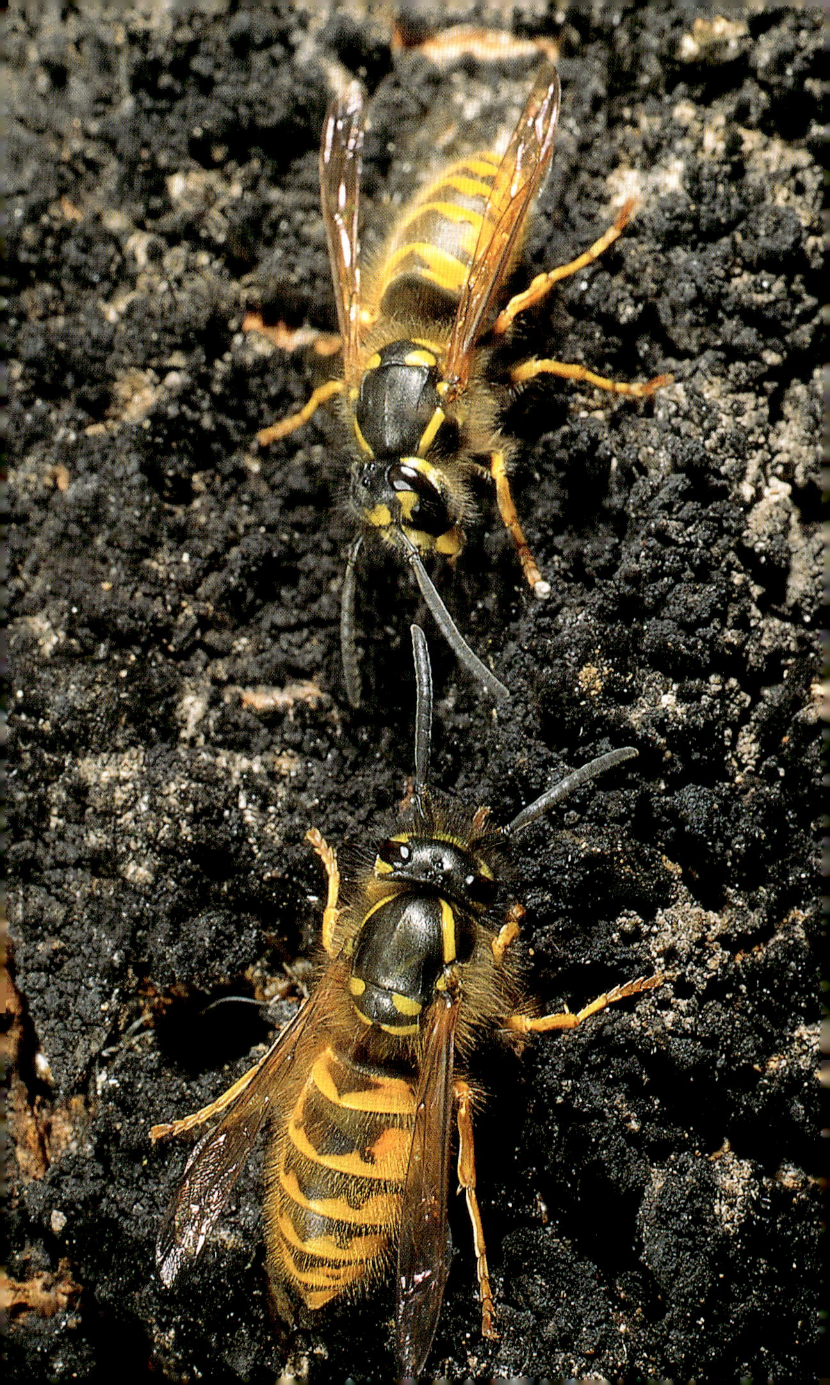

Australian Paper Wasp/Pi Whero

52
Polistes tasmaniensis humilis Order: HYMENOPTERA
Family: VESPIDAE

Appearance • A slender, orange-brown wasp with a tapered abdomen, a typically slender 'wasp waist' and yellowish wings.

Development • A small, umbrella-shaped nest is built by the wasp, constructed out of 'paper' that is actually bark and wood shavings chewed up by the wasps. This is often built in sheltered areas such as under the eaves of buildings. The larvae are reared on insects collected by the adult wasps. The adults, however, feed on nectar.

Distribution and Habitat • Warmer parts of the North Island.

Adult body length • 12 mm.

Remarks • A second paper wasp has also become established in New Zealand. This is the Asian Paper Wasp, *Polistes chinensis*. It has the more typical wasp markings of black and yellow stripes.

Paper wasps are capable of giving a nasty sting with relatively little provocation.

Honey Bee/Pi Honi
Apis mellifera

Order: HYMENOPTERA
Family: APIDAE

53

Appearance • A medium-sized bee. Its abdomen is striped in buff and yellow and it has specialised, basket-like structures on its hindlegs in which it carries the pollen it collects.

Development • Eggs are laid in special wax brood cells. Drones develop from unfertilised eggs and their sole function is to fertilise the queen, after which the workers either kill them or drive them out of the hive. Queens and workers develop from fertilised eggs, the queens produced by feeding selected larvae with royal jelly.

Distribution and Habitat • Domesticated Honey Bees occur in hives throughout the country to moderate altitudes. Sometimes wild hives are established by swarming bees, usually in forested areas.

Adult body length • 12 mm.

Remarks • A network of wax cells is constructed to store honey in. They are also used to raise the bee larvae.

Bees communicate by means of 'dance', with information being conveyed with stylised movements.

Honey Bee worker.

Bumblebee/Pi Rorohua
54 *Bombus terrestris*

Order: HYMENOPTERA
Family: APIDAE

Appearance • Conspicuous plump body with a broad yellow band at the front of the thorax and on the abdomen. Abdominal tip is also yellow.

Development • All Bumblebees, except for the queens which hibernate, die off at the advent of colder weather. In spring the queen emerges and builds a nest, usually in holes in the ground or in trees, sometimes in other places such as in rubble or vegetation. As they emerge, the larvae help the queen to feed later arrivals.

Distribution and Habitat • In pasturelands throughout New Zealand but less common at higher altitudes.

Adult body length • 24 mm.

Remarks • Also called Humblebees.

There are four species of Bumblebees in New Zealand: *Bombus terrestris*, *B. hortorum*, *B. ruderatus* and *B. subterraneus*. They can be separated by their differing striped patterns. Although originally introduced from Britain, some of these species are now extinct there.

All four species have tongues of differing lengths for harvesting different foods. Ironically, those with the longest tongues, *Bombus subterraneus* and *B. hortorum,* have the shortest tempers. Usually placid, when riled they emit a loud and angry buzz.

Bumblebees are important pollinators of plants such as clover.

Bumblebee worker.

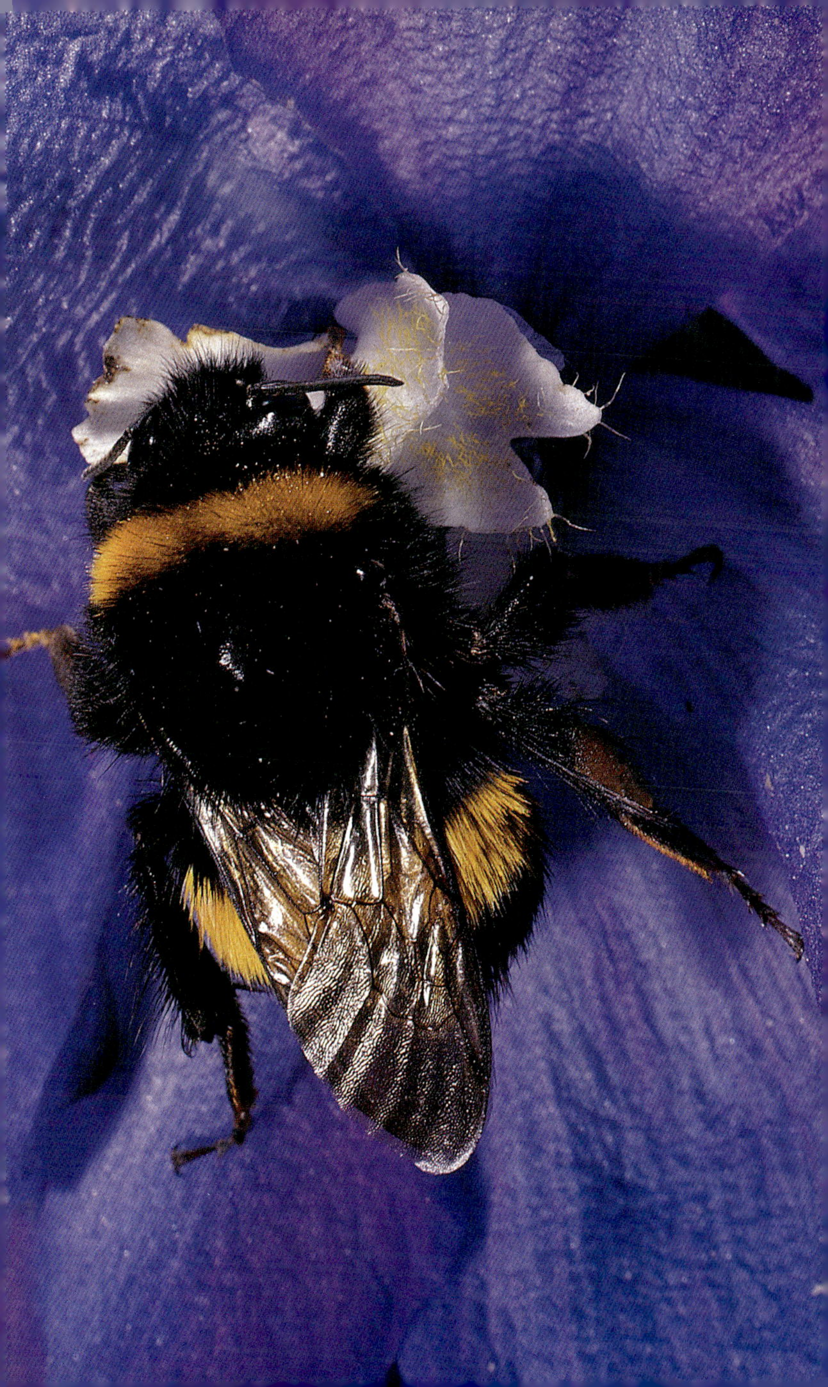

55 Southern Ant/Upokoru
Monomorium antarcticum

Order: HYMENOPTERA
Family: FORMICIDAE

Appearance • A tiny, usually wingless, rapidly moving insect, with its thorax and abdomen joined by a thin 'wasp-waist'. Has bent antennae. It can range in colour from black to bright orange with darker markings.

Development • An ant colony is made up of three castes: winged males and females; queens, which are fertilised females that have discarded their wings; and workers, which are sterile females that do the bulk of the work. This work is mainly feeding the ant larvae and the queen and keeping the ant nest hygienic.

Distribution and Habitat • Throughout New Zealand from lowland to upland areas.

Adult body length • 3 mm.

Remarks • Ants are gregarious insects, forming colonies in favoured areas like rotting logs or underground. They maintain elaborate societies composed of various castes, each caste filling its own particular function, such as food gathering or defence of the colony.

Our commonest ant, the Southern Ant, does not usually enter dwellings. The ants which invade houses are usually exotic species like the White-footed Ant, *Technomyrmex albipes*, Pharaoh's Ant, *Monomorium pharaonis*, or the Oriental Ant, *M. orientale*.

Native ants that you may come across are the Striated Ant, *Huberia striata*, and the Red Ant, *Mesoponera castanea*. Further, in the Auckland region, the recently arrived Argentine Ant, *Linepithema humile*, is causing concern, as it kills or displaces native animals.

Southern Ant queen.

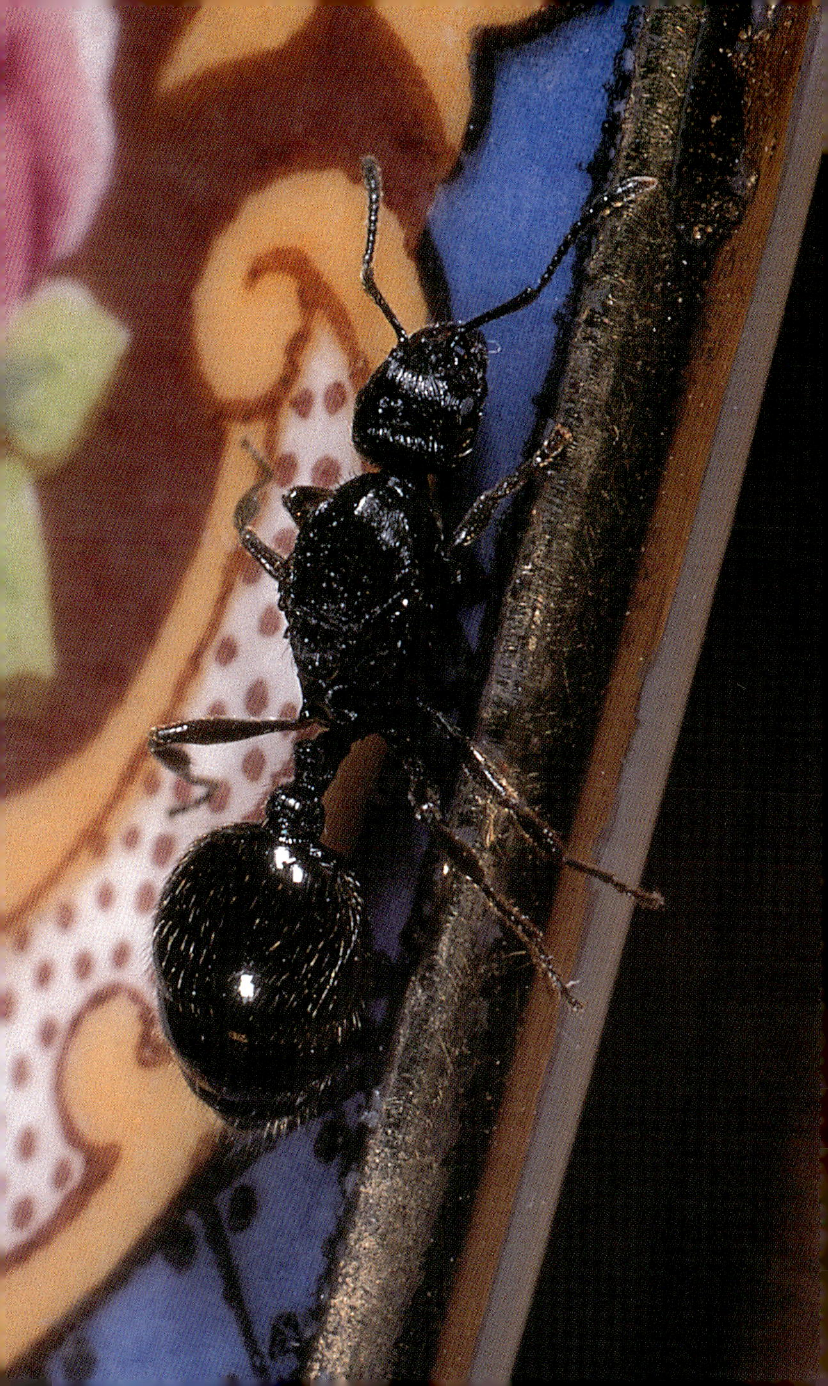

Index of common names

Note: numbers refer to Species No.

Antlion 28
Auckland Tree Weta 13
Australian Damselfly 2
Australian Paper Wasp 52
Australian Soldierfly 42
Backswimmer 19
Black Cockroach 7
Black Field Cricket 15
Blue Damselfly 3
Bumblebee 54
Bush Giant Dragonfly 5
Cabbage Aphid 21
Caddisfly 46
Carabid Beetle 29
Cat Flea 39
Cave Weta 14
Clapping Cicada 20
Click Beetle 35
Common Copper 49
Common Wasp 51
Cosmopolitan Diving Beetle 30
Crane Fly 43
Devil's Coachhorse Beetle 31
Dobsonfly 27
Elephant Weevil 37
European Earwig 11
German Wasp 50
Giraffe Weevil 38

Gisborne Cockroach 8
Golden-haired Blowfly 44
Green Vegetable Bug 22
Greenhouse Thrip 26
Honey Bee 53
Huhu Beetle 34
Katydid 16
Large Green Stonefly 6
Manuka Beetle 33
Migratory Locust 17
Monarch Butterfly 48
New Zealand Blue Blowfly 45
Passionvine Hopper 23
Praying Mantis 9
Prickly Stick Insect 18
Redcoat Damselfly 4
Sandfly 41
Shore Earwig 12
Southern Ant 55
Spiny-gilled Mayfly 1
Springbok Mantis 10
Steelblue Ladybird 36
Tiger Beetle 32
Vigilant Mosquito 40
Waterboatman 25
Watermeasurer 24
White Butterfly 47

Index of Maori names

Hoe Tuara   19
Hoehoe Tuara   25
Kahuka   48
Kakapowai   5
Kapakapa   17
Kekerengu   7
Kekerewai   33
Kekewai   3
Kihikihi wawa   20
Kihitara   4
Kikipounamu   16
Kiri Wenua Kakariki   22
Kui   32
Kurikuri   29
Kutukutu   28
Mata   12
Matua Waeroa Rere   43
Mokarakare   49
Mumutawa   36
Namu   41
Ngaro Parirau   27
Ngaro Waiwai   46

Ngarongaro Wai   6
Pepe Ma   47
Pepe Tunga   34
Pi Honi   53
Pi Rorohua   54
Pi Whero   52
Pihareinga   15
Piri Wai   1
Puruhi   39
Rango Pango   45
Rango Tuamaro   44
Ro   18
Tiemiemi   2
Tokoriro   13
Tupanapana   35
Tuwhaipapa   38
Upokoru   55
Waeroa   40
Wahipi   50, 51
Wai Tataka   30
Weta Taipo   14
Whe   9

Index of scientific names

Acanthoxyla prasina   18
Amphipsalta cingulata   21
Anisolabis littorea   12
Anisops assimilis   19
Apis mellifera   53
Archichauliodes diversus   27
Austrolestes colensonis   3
Austrosimulium australense   41
Bombus terrestris   54
Brevicoryne brassicae   21
Caedicia simplex   16
Calliphora laemica   44
Calliphora quadrimaculata   45
Coloburiscus humeralis   1
Conoderus exsul   35
Creophilus oculatus   31
Ctenocephalides felis   39
Culex pervigilans   40
Danaus plexippus   48
Drymaplaneta semivitta   8
Exaireta spinigera   42
Forficula auricularia   11
Gymnoplectron spp.   14
Heliothrips haemorrhoidalis   26
Hemideina thoracica   13
Holorusia novarae   43
Hydrobiosis parumbripennis   46
Hydrometra risbeci   24

Ischnura aurora aurora   2
Lasiorhynchus barbicornis   38
Locusta migratoria   17
Lycaena salustius   49
Megadromus capito   29
Miomantis caffra   10
Monomorium antarcticum   55
Neocicindela tuberculata   32
Nezara viridula   22
Orcus chalybeus   36
Orthodera novaezealandiae   9
Pieris rapae   47
Platyzosteria novaeseelandiae   7
Polistes tasmaniensis humilis   52
Prionoplus reticularis   34
Pyronota festiva   33
Rhantus pulverosus   30
Rhyncodes ursus   37
Scolypopa australis   23
Sigara arguta   25
Stenoperla prasina   6
Teleogryllus commodus   15
Uropetala carovei   5
Vespula germanica   50
Vespula vulgaris   51
Weeleus acutus   28
Xanthocnemis zealandica   4